Penguin Books
The Decline and Fall of the Middle Class

Patrick Hutber has been City Editor of the *Sunday Telegraph*
since 1966. Born in 1928, he was educated at Ealing County
Grammar School. At the age of seventeen he won a
Galsworthy Scholarship to New College, Oxford, and after
National Service in Germany he went up to Oxford in 1948,
reading English Language and Literature. Active in student
politics, he was successively Secretary and Librarian of the
Oxford Union.

After a period in industry he went to the Institute of Bankers
in 1954 and then, in 1957, to the *Financial Times*, where he
was trained by Gordon Newton. Over a six-year period he
was feature writer, Commercial Editor, leader writer and
finally writer of the 'Lex' stock market column. He then
spent three years as a financial consultant (during which
time he started the 'Questor' column in the *Daily
Telegraph*) before joining the *Sunday Telegraph*. In 1972 he
received the Senior Wincott Award as Financial Journalist
of the Year. He is editing *What is Wrong With Britain?*

Patrick Hutber lives in Buckinghamshire, is married and has
four children.

Patrick Hutber

The Decline and Fall of the Middle Class

– and how it can fight back

Penguin Books

Penguin Books Ltd, Harmondsworth,
Middlesex, England
Penguin Books, 625 Madison Avenue,
New York, New York 10022, U.S.A.
Penguin Books Australia Ltd, Ringwood,
Victoria, Australia
Penguin Books Canada Ltd, 2801 John Street,
Markham, Ontario, Canada L3R 1B4
Penguin Books (N.Z.) Ltd, 182–190 Wairau Road,
Auckland 10, New Zealand

First published by Associated Business Programmes 1976
Published with revisions in Penguin Books 1977

Made and printed in Great Britain by
Hazell Watson & Viney Ltd,
Aylesbury, Bucks
Set in Monotype Times Roman

TO THE MEMORY OF MY MOTHER
IN LOVE AND GRATITUDE

Contents

Introduction

There is certainly nothing new in the middle classes in Britain feeling themselves under pressure. They did so after the First World War, and to a much greater degree after the Second. But the period since 1974 is, perhaps, the first one during which they have felt and known themselves to be under attack. When Roy Lewis and Angus Maude published their classic *The English Middle Classes* in 1949 they were able to report in their final chapter that 'the attitude of the middle classes towards the future is much what the attitude of the individual middle-class bread-winner always is: an amalgam of dread and confidence'. I do not think that if they were writing today, they would be able to use those words. Dread there may be, anger there is coming to be, but of confidence there is almost none. That this is a time of crisis for the nation is a commonplace, but it is equally a time of crisis for the middle classes, who are subjected to unprecedented pressures and, at the same time, to unprecedented denigration.

Part of the purpose of this book is to suggest that the two crises are interlinked. Its main object, however, is to bring aid and comfort to the beleaguered. Back in 1949, Lewis and Maude could permit themselves an attitude of sympathetic detachment to their subject. They were writing a sociological study. This book is not so much about as for the middle classes. It discusses who they are and why they matter, as any work on the topic must. Its main theme is how they got themselves into their present plight and how they may get themselves out of it, if they choose to do so. I hope that much of the advice it contains is practical, but I also hope that the chapters on what has gone wrong will prove the most useful of all. The causes of the decline of the middle classes are to be found in politics, in economics, in social trends and in certain characteristics and tendencies of the middle classes themselves. Never has a section of society more enthusiastically co-operated in its own euthanasia.

I am not a determinist. I believe that political and social trends can be changed and economic problems overcome. But I am sure that the middle classes will not be able to reverse the process of their decay unless they are very clear what is happening and how far they have contributed, and are still contributing to their own downfall. Above all, I hope to hearten people. If the first stage in the fight back is to understand what has been happening, the next is to realize that the process can be put into reverse, and the third. to know that this would be desirable, not only for individuals, but for the nation as a whole. Inevitably, therefore, the book is a blend of explanation, exhortation and practical advice, but it could well be that the exhortation is the most important part of it.

I have to declare a personal interest. I was born into a middle-class family, my father a civil servant, my mother a doctor's daughter. (In case this should conjure up a false image of smugly insensitive security, I must add that my mother was widowed in 1945. At that time civil servants' widows did not receive pensions, so that until she reached the age of sixty she received a 10s. pension, from which 3s. 4d. had to be deducted for a national insurance stamp. In spite of this she saw I went to Oxford.) I spent the first twenty-five years of my life in Ealing, once known as Queen of the Suburbs, and surely, even today, a quintessentially middle-class place. Journalists have a social mobility that is peculiar to their occupation, either as members of the Fourth Estate or of the '*classe des déclassés*'. But for all the fact that on the lips of the ignorant the word 'suburban' is almost as pejorative as the phrase 'middle class' itself, I derive a warmth and comfort from that background. How strange that I should have thought it necessary to write the preceding sentence. Nobody would regard it as being in the least unusual or out of the way for someone with a working-class background to pay tribute to what it had given him. That it is, alas, more unusual to praise a suburban home rather than, say, a back street in Leeds is an indication of how thoroughly we have all been brainwashed. That this book may be a first step, however small, in reversing this deep indoctrination is my earnest wish.

The table of contents is, I hope, self-explanatory. Part I discusses the decline. Part II is devoted to the fight back, whether in the little things of life like dealing with bureaucracies, the not so little, like dealing with the taxman, or the big things, like organizing for a change of political course.

A number of friends have read and commented on various parts of the manuscript. I am particularly grateful to Dr E. Nelson, Mr John Gorst, M.P., and Mr G. K. Embleton for comments on Chapters 1, 9 and 12 respectively. Mr Ralph Harris, Mr T. Y. Benyon and Mr R. G. Miles made most helpful suggestions, while Mr Samuel Brittan read most of the manuscript in draft. Both mistakes and opinions are, of course, my responsibility alone.

I have to thank *The Economist* for permission to reproduce material on p. 50 and p. 65, and Mr James Morrell of the Henley Centre for Forecasting for permission to use the table on p. 17. Thanks are also due to Mr Norman St John Stevas, M.P., and Mr Leon Brittan, M.P., for permission to make use of material from their pamphlet 'How to Save Your Schools'. Mrs B. Doherty typed like one possessed in order to get the manuscript ready on time.

I should add that Mr Healey's habit of having a Budget every three months or so – and then making his tax changes conditional on T.U.C. reaction – makes it almost impossible to keep wholly up-to-date where tax rates are concerned. The figures in this book are accurate as at March 1977.

PART ONE
The decline

1 Who are the middle classes?

The question asked in the title of this chapter is, it has to be admitted, a strikingly unoriginal one, but it is, surely, where we should begin. If the question is unoriginal that is because it has been asked so many times, without a truly satisfactory answer ever really being given. As Lewis and Maude say, 'No one has ever found a definition of the English middle classes which is short, satisfactory, and watertight.'[1] I doubt whether a long answer has been found either, and yet without a definition we can get nowhere. At the very lowest, we must have some idea whom we are writing about; it is hardly possible to take up the cudgels on behalf of a wholly undefined group. Moreover, the mere lack of definition has, in a strange way, damaged the middle classes in the past. It is much easier to portray them as a snobbish, selfish minority if one carefully avoids the necessity of asking who they are and what proportion of the population they represent.

The most systematic attempts at definition have come, as might be expected, from the pollsters and market researchers. They talk, in a phrase redolent, according to taste, either of scientific objectivity or of the most exquisite embarrassment, of socio-economic groups, which represent attempts to grade the population on the basis of occupation and status. The groups range from Group A, professional, senior managerial and executive, down to the DE groups, those mainly dependent on state retirement pensions and government assistance for their income.

There are a number of difficulties with this type of approach. Historically speaking, the pollsters are concerned for easily understandable reasons with spending power. Their bread and butter, and most of their jam, comes from defining the directions in which advertising and marketing campaigns should be directed. The earlier post-war groupings in fact tended to be in terms of income. This was quickly found to be unsatisfactory and the definitions are now usually made in terms of occupation. This in itself gives rise to a number of oddities. One is that it is the occupation of the head of the household that counts; in the strict Victorian world of the market researchers, women who marry beneath them are immediately *déclassée*. And the lowest group of all groups, those with no earning capacity, may include many elderly widows who, by origin and marriage, would certainly be regarded as middle class, though if they have a pension from their husband they can be reclassified. Then there is the question of occupations. One such classification gives the following results:

1. Managerial, executive and professional.
2. Lower middle class, nurses, clerks, laboratory assistants, etc.
3. Skilled manual workers, including foremen and senior shop assistants.
4. Non-skilled manual workers and those mainly dependent on state retirement pensions and assistance for their income.[2]

This suggests that occupation is not in itself necessarily much more reliable than income. Some occupations are incontestably middle class – one thinks of doctors or solicitors. There is equally little difficulty in categorizing coal-miners or dustmen as working class. Other cases are much more difficult. Nursing draws recruits from all sections of the community; there are not a few successful entrepreneurs in, for example, the building trade who are incontestably working class, not just in origin and speech but in their life-style. Some sociological surveys indeed tie themselves in the most delightful knots. One such classifies farmers with over 500 acres as the highest grade, farmers with 100–500 acres as lower managerial or administrative, farmers with thirty to thirty-nine acres as skilled or supervisory non-manual.[3] This last is the lowest middle-class group in this particular study so that, presumably, a farmer or small-holder with twenty-nine acres is automatically working class. So much the worse for any retired officers who set themselves up on the land.

However, a start has to be made somewhere. The most recent re-working of these commercial, market research classifications[4] gives the results shown in Table 1:

TABLE 1

Label	Typical occupations of head of household	Approx. % of all adults
AB	'A's – senior hospital consultant, university professor, barrister, director of public or large private company, civil servant in senior administrative grade. 'B's – the range just below, e.g. junior consultant, general practitioner, newly called barrister, young director or senior manager in industry or commerce, civil servant up to 'Principal' level.	14
C1	Small shopkeeper (own shop), less senior manager in industry or commerce, senior bank clerk, senior nursing grades, executive branch civil servants.	22
C2	All skilled manual occupations and some lower-grade 'white-collar' workers, e.g. engine driver, plumber, welder, shop assistant. Usually have had apprenticeship or other formal training.	32
DE	'D's – all in unskilled manual occupations, e.g. farm labourer, plumber's mate, unskilled factory worker, window cleaner. 'E's – old age pensioners with no other income source, those (e.g. invalids) with no earning capacity whose standard of living is just above subsistence level.	32

According to this classification, the working class composes some 64 per cent of the population, which gives 36 per cent as the percentage for the middle and/or upper classes.

A 1966 classification makes the split 68 per cent–32 per cent, while Mark Abrams in 1964 puts the figures at 70 per cent–30 per cent. One would like to think that this indicated a progressive enlarging of the middle classes, but it is more likely to be a question of difference of methods. Still, it does give us a start. The best the market research classifiers have done, drawing upon the fruits of sociological research, gives us a figure of 36 per cent for the middle and/or upper classes.

One side-effect of inflation is to destroy previous rough correlations between income and social class. As a result market researchers have dropped income level altogether from their classifications and rely entirely on the occupation of the head of the household. Except at the absolute extremes of the scale – and not always even then – it is no longer possible to deduce anyone's social class from the income he or she receives.

There are, fortunately, other possible means of definition. One is by exclusion. If one deducts from a total population of around fifty-six million all those who are not middle class, taking, as one must, the family as the unit of definition, then one is left with the middle classes. From the point of view of seeing the problem clearly, this has certain advantages. The first step would be at the top end of the scale to exclude the upper class. One has only to say this to realize that this involves only a very few thousand people. The hereditary aristocracy certainly, but not life peers. The feature of this new form of ennoblement is that it enables beneficiaries to enter the House of Lords without leaving their own social class. Many life peers are completely middle class; another large and useful group of them are wholly and rightly working class. To the peerage one can add the diminishing category of the landed gentry. The numbers are small. In addition, though it is often claimed from the left that the class structure of this country is virtually intact, we have surely witnessed the virtual abdication of the upper class over the past thirty years. When Mr John Gorst, M.P., decided to form his Middle Class Association, he wrote a large number of letters to likely people asking for support. Of all the recipients only two or three replied that while sympathetic, they were ineligible to join as they were not middle class but upper class. Most people, told this small story are, as Mr Gorst was, both amused and surprised – surprised, that is, that there are still people today publicly laying claim to upper-class status. But, if we take a step back, the surprising thing is not that members of the upper class, if it exists, should acknowledge their status. It is that, when they do so, this should be a subject for amused comment.

There are not many people, then, to be excluded at the top end of the scale. This fact in itself is of very great significance. There are a very large number of different ways of looking at society. One is a three-class system – upper, middle, lower – indeed, the very name middle class is almost a nonsense if there is nothing to be in the middle of. A three-class system lends itself very readily to being combined with a model that divides the population into two groups – the oppressed and the oppressors. In this sort of picture, the middle classes are sandwiched uneasily between, looking down on the workers but sharing in their exploitation. If there is no significant upper class this model becomes more difficult to sustain. After all, there have to be people to do the oppressing and the oppressors are presumably buried in some substructure of the middle class. Let no one under-estimate the importance of even this slight shift. At the February 1974 election, for example, the Labour Party called in its manifesto for 'a fundamental and irreversible shift of power and wealth in favour of working people and their families'. If I am right in suggesting that this is a two-class nation, then that shift can only be from, and at the expense of, the middle class.

This leaves the question of who is to decide who is middle class and who working class. I have already suggested that the sociology of the market researchers does not provide an altogether satisfactory basis. In newly Communist countries it is decided – and drastically – by the state. As Raymond Postgate points out, 'For decades citizens of Russia and satellite countries who had belonged to the middle or upper classes were placed under deliberate disadvantages, in education and everything else, in order to make sure they were pushed down to the level of the mass, or even below.'[5] In order to stand a chance of higher education, for example, you had to prove that your parents were of worker or peasant origin. The decision is, or was – the position is said to be easing now – presumably taken by a bureaucrat, just as in South Africa another sort of bureaucrat rules whether a doubtful case is to be considered white, coloured or black. But if the decision is not to be taken on some arbitrary basis by an official – and, thank heavens, we do not yet have a Ministry of Class Status – then we are thrown back on some system of self-assessment. From time to time the opinion polls ask a sample of the population to say which social class they consider they belong to. In one immediate post-war poll[6] the results came out as follows:

Upper	2%
Upper middle	6%
Middle	28%
Lower middle	13%
Working	46%
No reply	5%

The immediately significant feature of these figures is that the number of people regarding themselves as middle class is larger (47 per cent) than the number regarding themselves as working class (46 per cent). No split of the don't knows would be likely to change this result very far.

The Gallup Poll has continued to ask similar questions at intervals, using samples of varying size. One illuminating poll, using a relatively large sample, dates from the time of the general election in October 1974. The replies at this time were as follows:

Upper	0·3%
Upper middle	2·3%
Middle	30·9%
Lower middle	11·6%
Working	49·0%
Don't know	5·9%

The similarities between this and the previous poll are, taken with a quarter of a century between them, perhaps more significant than the differences. The upper class (2 per cent in the first poll) has dwindled to a numerically insignificant fraction of a percentage point. And the split comes out as 49 per cent perceiving themselves as working class against 44·8 per cent perceiving themselves as middle class.

It could be held that letting people assess themselves is even more unsatisfactory than having the job done by a panel of sociologists. On this view, the results contain a large element of wishful thinking. This again, if so, is a fact that should not be ignored. The bias is presumed to be working-class people wishing to be middle class, not middle-class people wishing to be thought working class, and if, after all that has happened in the past sixty years, a large section of the working class wishes to be middle class, then the middle classes might derive some hope from this. The surveys, however, are far from valueless. If we accept this built-in bias (and, human nature being what it is, it would be foolish not to), then the method of self-assessment provides us with an upper limit.

However, there is a further complication which, at this stage, we have to take into account. Recent work by one leading research firm suggests that people do not always assess themselves in exactly the same way, and, more surprisingly, that how they assess themselves depends on the degree of consumer confidence.[7] Table 2 shows that even between January 1974 and October 1974 there was a perceptible change in the way people rated their parents' origins, their own standing and their eldest child's destination. Significantly, too, more people think that their children will be middle class than think themselves middle class. But these points, though fascinating, do not affect our main conclusion.

There are almost certainly less middle-class people than the number who categorize themselves as such. There are certainly not more. In the same way, there are almost certainly more middle-class people than the categories of the marketing surveys suggest. There are certainly not less.

By this simple means, therefore, we arrive at a lower limit of one third and an upper limit of one half of the population for the middle classes. (In this first chapter, I am using the slightly pedantic phrase 'middle classes' to emphasize that there is not a homogeneous group, but great variety and diversity in middle-class patterns and groups. This point made, I shall use the simpler, less accurate but less pedantic phrase 'middle class' in the rest of the book.) To my mind it is mildly surprising to do the sum, simple though it is. Phrases such as 'the mass of the people' condition us to think of a vast mass of 'workers', with the middle classes by comparison a tiny, if highly privileged minority. The

TABLE 2

	January 1974 (%)	*October 1974* (%)
My parents were:		
upper class	1	*less than* 1
upper middle	5	4
middle	22	21
lower middle	9	8
upper working	14	15
working	41	43
lower working	5	4
I am:		
upper class	1	*less than* 1
upper middle	5	4
middle	29	27
lower middle	12	12
upper working	18	19
working	34	35
lower working	1	1
My eldest child will be:		
upper class	1	1
upper middle	8	8
middle	30	28
lower middle	11	11
upper working	14	16
working	15	17
lower working	1	1

reality is very different. Somewhere in the region of half the population is middle class. Any irreversible shift of power and wealth towards working people and their families is clearly going to be at the expense of the middle classes. The very phrase 'working people', unlike the older, gentler phrase 'workers by hand and brain', is clearly designed to exclude middle-class people from the definition. On these figures, therefore, a little more than one half the nation is invited to plunder a little less than one half the nation.

One of the questions we shall have to ask later is how so large a section of the community as the middle classes appears to be lain so low and to demonstrate so little political muscle. But to calculate how many middle-class people there are brings us no nearer an answer to the question at the start of this chapter. One can reluctantly put on one side the joke definitions; Lewis and Maude, for example, suggested that, before the war, the middle classes could be held to comprise all those who used napkin rings. The upper class used a clean napkin at each meal and the working class did not use table napkins at all. As for the dividing line between the upper and the lower middle class, this came at the point at which a napkin became a serviette. One can run through occupations (where are farmers to be put?), through incomes (where do distressed gentlefolk come?), through education, through speech patterns (where does one classify David Frost?), and feel tempted to say that a member of the middle classes is like an elephant – one knows it when one sees it. That, of course, is not good enough, which is why I would suggest an alternative definition, that of motivation.

If a single word had to be found to sum up the characteristic middle-class virtues, middle-class aspirations and middle-class attitudes, I would choose a relatively old-fashioned one: thrift. Put in a slightly longer, slightly more up-to-date phrase, it could be called the readiness to postpone satisfactions. Deeply imbued with the Puritan ethic, the middle classes in Britain have always been hard-working; in contrast to Germany before the Weimar inflation, the proportion of the population existing as *rentiers* on investment income has been tiny. But they have also been thrifty, and thrift represents no more and no less than a readiness to postpone a satisfaction today in order to enjoy a greater one at some time in the future. The middle classes are the saving classes, whether their aim is to build up a business, provide a nest-egg or pension for their old age, buy a house to live in or leave some provision for their children.

To do this, they have given up many immediate pleasures. Characteristically, it is the middle-class parents who will sacrifice for their children's education, while the child itself, imbued with middle-class values, is prepared to postpone the satisfactions of financial independence throughout a prolonged period of dependence.

Equally, the characteristic middle-class attitude would be to regard it as normal to own one's house and to make as much provision as possible for one's own retirement. Consequently, from this primary belief in thrift a number of other attitudes stem. There is certainly an orientation towards money, because the middle classes are interested in the things that money will buy. To those who regard the love of money as the root of all evil, this is sufficient to condemn them out of hand. There is equally a belief in, a desire for, independence and as a consequence, a prejudice in favour of independence, an obstinate belief that it is natural to stand on one's own two feet.

The characteristic working-class attitude is very different from this. It starts from a different frame of mind, a reluctance to postpone satisfaction that may well arise from a time when such precarious pleasures as were available to the working class had to be snatched at as and when the opportunity arose. The satisfaction is taken today. The habit, or legend, of the traditional northern family priding itself in spending every farthing of its holiday money and laying on the mantelpiece just enough to pay for the taxi home, is revealing on this score; even when something is saved for, there is a positive pride in spending every penny, which is equated with extracting the last ounce of satisfaction from the holiday. (This may, in fact, explain why it is that the only possessors of very high incomes who are, in general, not subject to criticism or attack are pop singers and musicians. Their income in general tends to be spent, and conspicuously spent, not saved.) Again, from this primary belief a number of other attitudes stem. There is much less belief in self-reliance, much less desire for independence, or belief in its possibility and, as a consequence, a belief that it is natural and good for the state to care for an individual in retirement or at moments of crisis in life.

To draw this distinction is not to suggest for a moment that half the nation never saves, or that the other half always does. What we are writing of is tendencies and attitudes. Where the working class does save, it is much more likely to be for a specific short-term purpose. They are not so much saving as 'saving up' for a specific purpose, whether it is a holiday, a colour television set or an expensive coat. It is saving for the long term that seems to be the key middle-class determinant.

I am trying at this point to describe what seem to me to be two great natural constituencies, not to praise one or denigrate the other. The archetypal working-class virtues are warmth, spontaneity, generosity and neighbourliness. The archetypal middle-class vices are reserve, aloofness, a certain self-righteousness that consciousness of independence brings. One thinks, if you like, of the suburban street, with people sheltering behind their privet hedges, unaware even of the name of someone living two doors away. If the working-class archetype can be regarded as tending towards fecklessness, the middle-class archetype may tend towards selfishness. But equally it is not unfair to recognize in the middle-class striving for independence and belief in the possibility of self-help and self-improvement, a set of attitudes in many ways more adult than the greater dependence, whether on trade union or the State, regarded as the working-class norm.

All this is an attempt to describe two ways of life, two habits of mind, two sets of assumptions. There is no suggestion, however, that these attitudes can be strictly correlated with income levels or rigid social groups. I suggested earlier that there could be working-class millionaires. It is certainly true that there are members of the working class sharing all the middle-class attitudes to thrift and members of the middle classes to whom the postponement of satisfactions is unknown. These two great constituencies overlap the normal class boundaries as defined by market research and sociology; they blend, they shade off into each other, but they are none the less real for that.

There is another way in which the characteristic attitudes of the middle class can be described and which, to my mind, does not contradict but supplements the description of them as the people who postpone their satisfactions. They are people who tend to be, in David Riesman's phrase, 'inner-directed' rather than 'other-directed'. They are, many of them, individualists. They pursue their goals essentially by individual action, as opposed to the working class which has tended, and still tends, to pursue its goals by collective action. Since this book has a severely practical purpose, this is not the place to delve into psychological typing, but it is worth pointing out that any psychoanalyst would recognize in the tendency to orderliness, to ambition, to the accumulation and retention of money and possessions, a consistent and easily recognizable character-type. But if anyone doubts that thrift is the key point, the limiting case, then I would quote a small, but intensely illuminating piece of evidence. In an article in the *New Statesman* shortly after the start of the Government's new anti-inflation policy which imposed a £6 a week limit on pay rises for a period of one year, Mr Jack Jones, General Secretary of the Transport and General Workers' Union, argued passionately that, as a longer-term policy, flat-rate, rather than percentage, increases were preferable. His main objection to reverting to percentage increases was that 'Not only would the top wage and salary earners always get cumulatively greater increases, but they would always improve their ability to create more income and wealth for themselves by investments of various types . . . In other words, they have the opportunity to save and increase their wealth which is denied the mass of working people.'[8]

These are most revealing words. Saving, which I have suggested is the ultimate middle-class virtue, is, to Mr Jones, something close to a crime. He is not objecting that better-off people will enjoy a higher standard of living, flaunt their wealth or engage in conspicuous consumption. His objection is that they will save and thus increase their wealth. Mr Jones is where he is because of his abilities but, above all, because he represents his members. He is the quintessence of their aspirations and their prejudices. Quite intuitively, he has illuminated the great divide.

2 How the middle class sees itself

It is one thing to form one's own view as to the essential character of the middle class or to report the views of sociologists, but it seemed to me a cross-check was desirable. I therefore inserted a small item in my regular column in the *Sunday Telegraph*, inviting middle-class readers to write to me specifically about their hopes, their fears and their finances.

I got a very large response – a bulging file of letters, many of them of a length that suggested that they had taken a considerable time to write. There are at least three reasons why they are not a scientific sample. First, because they are drawn from among readers of a single newspaper, though one with a very wide readership among the middle class; second, because anyone who actually writes to a newspaper is, by definition, untypical, since most people do not; and third, because it is people who feel aggrieved who are more likely to put pen to paper than those who feel contented and prosperous. Nonetheless, when all allowances have been made, there was enough that was thought-provoking in the letters to justify not just discussing them here, but using them as a check against the views expressed in my first chapter, which was written *before* any of the letters were received.

First, there is no doubt whatever that, in the view of the writers, being middle class is a state of mind, and the words that recur time and again are 'thrift', 'independence' and 'hard work'. One correspondent wrote:

Let me start with aspirations which for me as a family man in my fiftieth year with a splendid wife and two fine lads at college, are topped by a wish to continue a happy, healthy, unencumbered family life. I started work as a junior and after twenty-six years of normal working, sometimes with long hours, I became a director of my company. Which is as it should be. I hope my sons will have similar opportunities and enjoy their working lives as much as I do.

My wife has not been employed since the boys were born, but she works hard to keep the house clean and pleasant, and is engaged in voluntary work. I would like to keep a larger proportion of my earnings so that we could spend more on our leisure time, but we manage to live comfortably and are sufficiently well educated to appreciate the free things in life, such as the museums, libraries, birdlife, fields and hedgerows and so on. But the money we are allowed to retain I stoutly claim the right to spend as I like. If I want to spend it on education for my children (I didn't) or on providing for private medical treatment that is my affair. Just who the hell do they think they are to tell me what I can buy or what I cannot. I just want to run a sound business, providing steady employment, in a sound economy; to respect and be respected by neighbours, staff, friends and associates and, in short, to enjoy 'the liberty which is the luxury of the self-disciplined'.

I start with this, because it is both typical and untypical – typical in its robust and unselfconscious tone, untypical in that it is virtually the only one which is basically optimistic in tone. The writer expresses fears about the 'growth of crime, hooliganism, pornography, violent vandalism and terrorism', the growth of inflation and 'strangling controls', but he is sufficiently self-confident to think about taking an early retirement at fifty-five to start up a small business of some kind of his own. His investments, he adds, are modest but have depreciated by over 50 per cent since 1972 – before applying the effects of inflation. He ends, 'I want this country and its people to be decent, solvent and united in purpose. I believe millions of hands would be raised in agreement if someone would only take the trouble to find out.'

Much, much more typical are pessimists. There is the university professor who writes:

I have to leave because I can no longer maintain a reasonable living standard while performing my job as it ought to be carried out. I still have time to make a good life and career in a new country but I cannot afford to back Britain any longer. From January 1st, 1976 I take up a position as head of department in an overseas university at $34,000 a year. To have as much money after tax in this country as I shall have there, I would need an amount of around £22,500. My present salary is £6,700.

There is, too, the famous novelist, a name that would be recognized in most middle-class households, who found that, for three successive years, his income amounted, at first sight, to the very happy sum of £16,000 per annum. For three years he found he was virtually unable to write. It is not, he says, that he writes for money; simply that he found it impossible to involve himself in the work of writing, knowing that most of the proceeds would simply go in tax.

Then there is the correspondent who says:

I remember how my father thought in 1942 that he had made more than adequate provision for his wife's modest needs by leaving her £15,000 and £1,000 gross per annum. By 1960 Mother was having to chip away at her capital and by 1970 it was disappearing at such a speed as to make it non-existent by 1973, even though inflation was only beginning to enter double figures.

This same correspondent's letter provides a remarkable progression. It starts with a definition of the middle class which reads more like a hymn of praise:

The hallmarks of a middle-class family were [note the tense – P.H.]:

A sense of personal pride and a desire to be self-supporting.

An ability to exercise self-discipline.

A desire to improve one's position in the world and to provide a better education for the children.

The recognition that an increase in income would only come through hard work and enterprise.

A desire to own a house, to have one's own family doctor, to be able to afford private nursing facilities, to possess a motor cycle or a car.

To be able to provide the family with a holiday, be it only a week at a local coastal resort and to ease the burden of household chores through domestic help.

A clear concept as to what constituted the necessities and what constituted the luxuries of life.

A respect for property and other persons.

An aspiration towards culture.

The ability to distinguish between material and spiritual.

A code of personal conduct and personal judgement as to what is right and what is wrong – a judgement which was derived from religious faith.

A respect for law and order.

A pride in being British and an instinct for 'fair play'.

A sense of personal responsibility for the well-being of one's wife and family.

A spirit of patriotism.

The will to make financial provision for old age.

Recognition as to the virtues of thrift and insurance.

A respect for the voice of authority, be it authority born of age or position.

An aspiration towards gentlemanly behaviour.

An appreciation of good manners, politeness and courtesy.

A respect for the gentle sex.

But this same letter, after detailing the effects of inflation, taxation and so on concludes on an alarming note:

In evil moments one is tempted by the image of a society where militancy on the labour front is countered by the edict 'Work or starve', where individual acts of violence and terror are met by punishments of a primeval character. Evil moods can be swept aside in the cold light of day but what does abide is the deep sense of helplessness, the feeling of utter frustration, at being unable to do anything to improve the situation.

A similar note of anxiety sounds in the letter of a London woman:

It is my belief that the way things are going, the middle classes are doomed to a gradual extinction over the course of the next generation or two, and with their disappearance we shall have lost the last bulwark of democracy . . . so far the middle classes are managing to survive. But we are mainly living like the camel in the desert does on the fat stored in its hump.

A recurrent note was struck in a comment from a woman reader: 'I hope, desperately, to be able to leave my very small capital to my daughter and family, and not have to use it up in a last few miserable months' reluctant existence.'

Next a letter from someone whom the market researchers might exclude from their definition of middle class purely on grounds of income.

May I make the point that many people claim to be middle class when, to my way of thinking, they are no such thing. They are the ones who like to think they have 'got on', who are everlastingly engaged in that soul-destroying rat race, who do not care how many folk they trample on in the process, who boast about their possessions and their conquests in whatever sphere, who must always 'keep up with the

Joneses'. [This last I should have thought, for better or worse, a very middle-class characteristic – P.H.]

Then too, there are those who sneer at what they call 'middle-class values' without really having much idea what they are. What such people seem to mean is a kind of hypocritical respectability. The values of the true middle class are ones that no one need be ashamed to aspire to: personal integrity, a recognition of the worth of human dignity and decency, fair play, loyalty, a sense of proportion and therefore a sense of humour and an ability to laugh at oneself, independence of spirit, courage (perhaps even more on the moral than the physical plane), a love of tradition, a feeling for beauty. These are all qualities that need preserving and they are just those qualities that our enemies seek to destroy.

Now for personal details. For a start I would comment that when the middle classes come under discussion, those concerned nearly always ignore people like me, a single person with a low income, yet I am sure that there are thousands of us who can quite properly call ourselves middle class.

I am a retired social worker, formerly employed by a voluntary society so that I never enjoyed a large salary, and I still live in what was the family home. In order to do this, I have let off two rooms after having house improvement work and re-decoration done just over two years ago. In addition to my State pension, I have an occupational pension of £163 per annum which would have been more but I had to take part in a lump sum to pay off a bank overdraft and to provide bridging finance until I got my tenant, who pays £7·75 per week for rent and gas. My total income is therefore in the region of £23 a week.

My main items of expenditure are something like this:

	Approximate weekly figure
Gas, electricity and solid fuel	£4
Food	£4
Clothing	75p
Rates	£1·50
	(thanks to rebate)
Telephone	75p
Laundry	75p
Insurances	75p
Servicing of appliances	25p
Newspapers and magazines	£1
Church collection and charity donations	75p
	£14·50

I have omitted minor incidentals. Since spending so much on the home in 1973 I have not had to pay a lot in maintenance expenses, but next year this factor will have to be taken into account again. The amount I spend on holidays varies and this year is only about £25–£30 due to the fact that transport all the way has been provided. Normal transport expenses are not great as the local authority provides a concessionary bus pass. I avoid train travel wherever possible because of the exorbitant cost. I cut down on postage by such devices as delivering my electricity, gas and rates cheque by hand, putting the laundry cheque in with the laundry and the envelope containing my monthly milk cheque in the neck of a returned bottle. I write few letters now and from last year have cut down on my holiday postcards and Christmas card list.

I suppose I do quite well, considering my income would be regarded by trade unionists as being below the poverty line . . . I stay in this house because it is my home, because it is in a pleasant spot and well-served with trades people (I can still have my groceries and furniture delivered, the small man again), because it houses the family furniture which would not go into a modern semi or flat and which means a good deal to me because of its associations. Of course, none of this would be regarded by Big Brother as important, which is one reason why I am totally opposed to Big Brother.

That letter seems to me worth quoting, if for nothing else, for its pride and serenity, but from the mass of letters, taken together, two things stand out. The first is that the older the correspondent, the greater the degree of bitterness and sometimes of desperation.

Bank interest is now only 6½ per cent gross, with inflation raging at 29 per cent. It has become impossible to live on interest alone and the only way to survive is to use up the capital. I think people of my generation have had a very rough deal, living through two world wars and being brought up to recognize hard work and thrift as virtues. It is no wonder that we feel embittered, frustrated, and apprehensive of the future. We feel cheated by Governments who have sold us gilt-edged securities now worth half their face value and with a fraction of their original purchasing power . . . The only consolation for the elderly is that we have lived most of our lives and will not remain to be cheated for ever.

The sentiment contained in that last sentence is one that recurs frighteningly often in the letters. I know that, with increasing age, there comes a natural darkening of the horizons but it still chills me to have correspondents end, after a meticulous description of their declining circumstances, with the words, 'Aspirations: one only – not to live too long', or, more cheerfully, 'I hope to receive the "final" call before the roof falls in.'

The second point that emerges from the correspondence is that there is one tax felt by writer after writer to be totally unjust. It is the surcharge upon investment income, which means that above £1,000 per annum it is taxed at 45 per cent and above £2,000 a year at 50 per cent. All the other exactions of the Welfare State, it seems, can be borne, but this, above all, sticks in the gullet. Correspondent after correspondent makes the point that his savings came from income on which he had already paid tax. A retired consultant writes that the income element of his annuity is treated as unearned – an annuity he had bought because when he retired at the mandatory Health Service age for consultants of sixty-five none of his contemporaries had earned pensions on their salaries of as much as £1,000 per annum.

If one could choose only one single tax reform out of the many that are to be desired, I have no doubt that this would be incomparably the most popular.

The letters also illustrate the painful conflict arising between inflation and the inbuilt middle-class desire to save:

I am twenty-eight and earning nearly £4,000 per annum in insurance as a departmental head. My main worry is financial in that there seems no reasonable way to save for the future. Although I am placing £50 a month with a building society, I am acutely aware that this is being continuously eroded by inflation and although I could save more there seems no point in doing so.

Despite all the above, I also feel that not to save is wrong, as I may one day marry and will then need savings behind me.

Next, an example of financial planning wrecked by inflation.

I am sixty-four years of age and four years ago I was advised by my doctor to retire. My salary at the time was just below £5,000 per annum and I now receive a 'fixed' pension of £1,500 per annum.

When the blow occurred, I immediately examined my financial situation and at the time I decided that by avoiding luxuries, life would be tolerable well into the foreseeable future, which only goes to show how even a professional manager can be wildly adrift in his forecast!

My calculations were all based on an annual inflation rate of $4\frac{1}{2}$ per cent which reflected the previous fifty years or so, and by projecting my 1971 essential outgoings twenty years forward at $4\frac{1}{2}$ per cent (to be safe!) compounded I got that side of the balance.

Against this I plotted my estimated net income, based on the fixed pension, plus initially my N.H.I. sick pay and superseded at the appropriate time by my N.H.S. retirement pension, these latter amounts being assumed to increase by $4\frac{1}{2}$ per cent per annum. I topped off the income by the anticipated interest from investments to give a gross income for each of the years ahead.

It was apparent from the outset that although initially income slightly exceeded expenditure, within about four years the reverse would apply . . . However even by 1990 I should still be solvent and I felt reasonably content.

By mid 1972 there were signs that inflation might be more serious than seemed likely two years before and most of the financial experts were urging people to transfer their capital from fixed interest investments to Unit Trusts or the like, as 'a hedge against inflation'.

Put not your faith in experts! My wife and I transferred all but about £1,500 of our capital from the building society to Growth trust – approximately £6,000 worth.

The wizardry of Ted Heath, ably assisted by Joe Gormley and the Arabs, quickly reduced this amount to about £4,000, then Harold had a go and reduced it to about £1,800. Recent improvement has now brought it back to about £4,000 but it is galling to remember that, if we'd left the £6,000 in the care of the building society, it would now be worth about £7,400. Hedge against inflation!! Experts!!! Huh!

Coupling this financial disaster with the astronomical inflation we are suffering, it will be obvious that my 1971 arithmetic is now well adrift of reality and the suicide date is currently set at about 1983 . . . I am currently preparing a brochure for the sale of my present house.

That, at least, was a very cheerful suicide threat. Finally, a letter written with a kind of infectious gaiety that gave me a great deal of pleasure and I hope may similarly please the reader. I think it speaks for itself:

I am really writing this letter under false pretences. Strictly speaking, both my husband and I (!) are not middle class. We are professional class, which is slightly different, I think. I certainly have never thought of myself as middle class until recently – I was campaigning to keep our local Grammar schools (so far we are winning) when one of my few failures said 'It's alright for you middle-class mums!' I was a bit staggered.

I was born in a cotton town, in 1930 (timing!). My father was already out of work, my mother's mill closed while she was off work to have me, and never re-opened. For my first three years of life, I was brought up on the Dole. After that things improved and by the time I was six my father was on overtime and I was taking his evening meal to the mill in a basin with a cloth over it. He was making cotton duck and khaki-drill! (Let no one tell you the Baldwin Government was completely daft.) We blessed Herr Hitler! If the rest of England were still ignorant, we knew a war was coming!

But I have since come to the conclusion that middle-classness is a state of mind, rather than status. Ours is a town of owner-occupiers. Terraces of good, stone-built houses that will last for ever. My parents had paid off the mortgage during the 20s. They had saved. They owed no one for anything. My mother was the best manager God ever made and we never went short of food or clothes and we were clean! 'Soap and water cost nothing' was her motto! We were told to work hard at school and get out of 'the mill' – too chancy altogether. We were also told that, although there was no money to help lame ducks, no one would ask us to leave school and go out to earn so long as we won scholarships and paid our way to 'college'.

So I worked. I got a scholarship to the local Grammar. Later, a State Scholarship to university. This brought me more than my father earned in a year. My husband, who had an identical background, was four years ahead of me at the same Grammar. He is now a company director. I teach history and geography. We have a nice house in a nice neighbourhood. But it all depends on salary. Taxation and inflation make it impossible to save. Our daughter has just done very well in A-levels and has a university place. But we get next to no grant. So more money goes on her for the next three years. When we stop earning we will have nothing left. It will be back to the terraced house.

We have both worked very hard all our lives. It seems hard that the benefit should be only transitory. The old idea of each generation building for the foundation of the next is now impossible.

Why bother to make the effort? It is easier to subside onto the vast State feather-bed, for which there are fewer and fewer willing to work to maintain.

But I can still hear my mother saying disparagingly of people that we met – 'but they live in a council house'. In — that was the equivalent to the Poor House. There were not, nor still are, many council houses in —. They were the last resort of the shiftless.

The human urge to better oneself, to improve on previous generations, is at present being stifled. When I was canvassing for our petition about the Grammar schools, my most fervent supporters were from staunch Labour territory. Not only is it being made more difficult to 'better' oneself, it is also being made certain that one does not benefit from it. What hurts one family hurts the country. England at the present seems determined on suicide. Oh for the old Elizabethan ethic – if you can get on – good luck to you! When the individual did well – so did the country!

3 Taxation and redistribution

This chapter has a simple purpose. It is to show just how far the position of the middle class has deteriorated under the burden of an increasing weight of taxation, and just how far redistribution has gone in this country.

One of the great difficulties in writing about the financial position of the middle class is that no two people discussing the subject seem to be talking about the same things. On the one hand, there is a wealth of subjective evidence from people who feel themselves worse off, the architect, for example, who says that the British middle-class family is

... up against the wall. I haven't seen a play in London in two years. I only eat in restaurants on business. Can't afford the gardener once a week any more. You start adding it up and it amounts to a social revolution. I find myself making fewer phone calls, writing fewer letters and taking fewer trips. The cost of all these services has doubled in the past year.

On the other hand, you have a widespread assumption by the spokesmen for the working class in the form of the trade union leaders that, if sacrifice is to be called for in the national interest, then it is self-evidently true that, in the interests of fairness, 'the rich' are the people who should make it. One then discovers that the rich are defined as anyone earning some arbitrary figure which, in a number of recent pronouncements, has come down as low as £3,000 a year. Since the national average earnings in mid-1975 were around £50 a week or £2,600 a year, it is clear that the word 'rich' is being used in some very special sense. We are, in fact, getting into a Gilbertian situation in which someone earning, say, £4,000 a year and buying a house on a mortgage which absorbs one quarter of his income, not to mention rates, is classified as rich, while a family with, say, three wage-earners, earning respectively £50 a week, £30 a week and £18 a week, paying a council rent which I will set at the average figure of £5 a week, is included in the proletariat.

This is a total nonsense. It is using the word 'rich', with its connotations of the possession of wealth, to describe relatively modest differences in income. A good example of the pejorative use of the word 'rich' comes from the Royal Ascot race meeting in June 1975. At the time there was a strike of stable lads who picketed the entrance as the race-goers arrived. The commentator for Independent Television News contrasted feelingly the rich inside and the poor outside. No doubt there were some persons of considerable wealth there, but he never paused to consider whether there might not be a number of people of relatively modest means who would choose to go to Ascot, using part of their discretionary spending in this way because they enjoyed it – or that a good evening in a northern Working Men's Club might well cost as much as a day at the races. But even where the word is properly applied to possessions, we will not get very far unless we distinguish two senses: rich (A), possessing wealth sufficient to meet all likely requirements, and rich (B), possessing slightly more than the speaker or those whom the speaker seeks to represent.

This distinction is highly important in discussing middle-class affluence or the lack of it. For example, it is customary and, in some ways convenient in discussions on the distribution of wealth and incomes, to talk in percentage groups, the richest 1 per cent, the richest 10 per cent and so on. What is not realized is what extremely modest categories these represent. Consider incomes first. If we take 1972/3, then the top 1 per cent of personal incomes included everyone receiving an income of not less than £6,236 a year.[9] In 1973/4, the last year for which figures are available, the figure had risen to only £7,195.[10] Similarly in 1972/3, the top 10 per cent of incomes included everyone earning not less than £2,857 a year. The following year it had risen to a princely £3,260. Similar considerations apply where wealth is concerned. One is often told, for example – somewhat untruthfully, as we shall see – that the top 10 per cent of wealth-holders own no less than 70 per cent of the wealth of this country. Shocking inequality! But then, when one looks at the definitions, it turns out that the top 10 per cent are all those people who own wealth worth at least £10,600 and even the top 1 per cent need own no more than £44,000 apiece to qualify.[11] These figures are vitally important. They explain how it is that, when measures are taken to attack the rich, measures which many middle-class people themselves have applauded or even instigated, it is the broad mass of the middle classes themselves who suffer.

Unfortunately, there has been, until recently at any rate, a fairly widespread assumption on the part of those to whom complaints were addressed, that such complaints were part of the middle-class stock in trade. The politicians have ignored the pleas, the sociologists have tended to say that, since the middle class is mobile, it tends to feel insecure and this leads to moaning, almost as a way of life. John Raynor, for example, writing about middle-class incomes, has this to say:

Since the People's Budget of 1909, the demise of the middle classes has been the subject of perennial prophecy, and over the years it has been built into a myth compounded of the views that salaries always lag behind prices, that taxation hits them more severely than other groups, and that, together, these reduce incentives . . . despite the myths, the middle classes, it would seem, have done quite well for themselves over the last fifty years.[12]

He was writing, admittedly, in 1969, and using figures that stopped in 1960, which, I suppose, is one of the advantages of undertaking scholarly research. We have had, fortunately, published in 1975 the Initial Report of the Royal Commission on the Distribution of Income and Wealth, followed by a second report in 1976. The figures this contains still lag a little behind in that they go no further than 1973, but they enable us to see what has happened, and there is one happy accident that makes them very useful to our purpose. Since the top 10 per cent of personal incomes included at the time everyone earning not less than £3,260, it is a category very relevant to the middle classes.

Just what has happened to the middle classes in terms of income over the past thirty years? Statistics are not always one's favourite reading, but those given in the Royal Commission

Report are so thought-provoking and so germane to my argument, that it is worth looking closely at them.

In 1938/9, the top 10 per cent of income-earners received more than 40 per cent of pre-tax earnings, 40·5 per cent to be precise. By 1972/3 that percentage was down to 26·9 per cent. If we take income after tax, the top 10 per cent of income-earners in 1938/9 received 34·6 per cent of total incomes. By 1972/3 that percentage was down to 23·6 per cent. The year 1972/3 is highly significant in one other respect. It was the last year before inflation turned from being a nuisance into being a major menace. It is impossible to know for certain how it will have affected these figures, but Samuel Brittan in the *Financial Times* (31 July 1975) suggests that the post-war share of the top 10 per cent of income-earners might now be down to as little as 20 per cent. He also points out that, if this 'excess' share of the top 10 per cent were to be divided among the rest of the population, it would mean an extra once-for-all £4 a week for all, with nothing further to gain from 'redistribution'. It is equally true that if all incomes exceeding £3,000 a year were to be confiscated the result would be an extra £2 a week for the rest of the population.

Clearly then, if the aim of redistribution is to benefit those who are to receive rather than to disadvantage those who are to contribute, there is little that redistribution of incomes can do. What about the redistribution of wealth? Again the best guide we have is the Initial Report of the Royal Commission, though much of this report consists of an analysis of the inadequacy of the data and a plea for more research.

Let us start with the notorious and often quoted figures about the top 10 per cent of the population owning 70 per cent of the wealth, a figure guaranteed to arouse much indignation among those unaware of the fact that the top 10 per cent includes everyone with net assets of not less than £10,600. At first sight the Report seems to give some countenance to this allegation. According to the crude figures of the Inland Revenue, the top 10 per cent owned 72 per cent of the personal wealth in 1972. Dreadful! But stay. The Revenue assumes in reaching this figure that those outside the death duties net own no wealth at all. This means that, to accept the 72 per cent figure, you have to believe that there are 20 million adults in the country owning nothing whatsoever. Clearly this is a nonsense, and the Diamond Commission quickly made some complicated estimates, recalculated the figures and suggested that the top 10 per cent own, in fact, 67·3 per cent of the total personal wealth.

But this is only a beginning. If, as the Commission does, you make allowance for occupational pension rights (which surely are as much a form of wealth as money saved in the bank or a building society for one's old age) the percentage comes down to 63·9 per cent. It is at this point that the real action starts. For if it is just to include some estimate of the value of occupational pensions, then surely allowance should be made for the value of all those State pension entitlements. These, according to the Government Actuaries Department, have a staggering total value of 154,232 *million* pounds. Again, they have a value to the recipient; they may not be negotiable but they will certainly increase the beneficiary's disposable wealth insofar as he does not have to save himself. According to the first Diamond Commission report accrued rights to State pensions were worth an average of £2,955 per head to the male population, and an average of £4,494 per head to the female population. If this entitlement is included in the calculation of personal wealth, a very big change takes place. The percentage of personal wealth owned by the top 10 per cent comes down from 63·9 per cent to 45·7 per cent.

In assessing this figure, two points need to be taken into account. The first is the effect of age upon wealth. By this, I mean no more and no less than that if everyone started equal from scratch, then older people would tend to have more wealth than younger people, simply because they had tended to accumulate savings in one form or another throughout their lives. Indeed, in an iconoclastic study of wealth published in 1974 (*How Much Inequality?* by George Polanyi and John B. Wood, I.E.A., 1974) the authors suggest that, if the age factor were the only one making for inequality, then 10 per cent of the population would still own as much as 30 per cent of the wealth.

The second point is that on the showing of the Diamond Commission's second report the 72 per cent figure we started with is very much out of date. By 1974, calculated on the same basis, the figure had come down to 66 per cent. This the Commission ascribes mainly to the fall in Stock Exchange values between the two years. It is hard to believe that the rich will have got any richer since then, but equally it is important to remember that the 66 per cent is as inflated and unrealistic a figure as the original 72 per cent. The inclusion of pension rights brings it down very quickly to 41 per cent.

Clearly, therefore, though there are, as one would expect and as I would hope, some very rich individuals, the picture of 'gross inequalities of wealth' is not one that can be sustained in the sense, which surely is the only one that matters, that most would have significantly more if only some had significantly less. Moreover, the steady trend over the decade has been towards greater equality. If we take that crude and unrealistic Inland Revenue figure of 72 per cent (and crude statistics deserve to be treated like crude sewage) of wealth in 1972 being owned by the top 10 per cent, the figure was down from 83 per cent in 1960, 88 per cent in 1938 and 92 per cent back in 1913 before the First World War.

Finally, we can look at the top 1 per cent who, in 1911, are estimated to have owned some 69 per cent of net personal wealth (again on the Inland Revenue 'crude' basis). By 1924–30 this was down to 62 per cent, by 1954 43 per cent, by 1960 42 per cent and by 1972 25·3 per cent. If you include pension rights in your estimates of wealth, the share of the top 1 per cent comes down to 14 per cent. Looking at the series of statistics as a whole, taking income as well as wealth, there are periods of exceptionally rapid change; 1949–59 was one such and 1972–5 is almost certainly another. There are periods when the pace of change has been slower, but the result has been that a very high degree of equality has been reached. Some of this process of change has been painless, or, at least, largely so. There has been, until very recently, a general and virtually continuous rise in overall living standards, which any sensible person will applaud and which has masked any relative middle-class decline. There has also been a substantial redistribution of income and wealth away from the middle classes, which has been by no means painless.

If neither the figures of the Diamond Commission nor the evidence of one's eye convince the reader, one simple example may, perhaps, do so. Let us consider the case of someone earning £1,000 a year before the last war, which one can accept as an amount that would sustain a comfortable, but hardly luxurious, middle-class existence. Inland Revenue figures shed some revealing light on this. In the tax year 1938–9 there were 290,000 people in the happy position of earning £1,000 or more before tax. By 1975 the cost of living had risen so much that £8,000 in 1975 was the bare equivalent of 1939's £1,000. The Inland Revenue figures show that in the tax year 1975–6 the number of people with a total income before tax of £8,000 and above was 490,000.

So far one might say splendid – it seems that quite a lot more people have reached this happy plateau. But then bring tax into the picture. Of the 290,000 earning more than £1,000 a year before the war, 215,000 were left with at least £1,000 a year *after tax*. Of the 490,000 in 1975 with £8,000 a year or more, there were only 85,000 left with the pre-war equivalent of £1,000 a year. Thanks to the operation of the taxation system, there has been, in spite of all the general rise in living standards, a drop of more than 60 per cent in the number of those enjoying this modest degree of affluence. And if one takes another figure, which is that in 1937 savings averaged 20 per cent of the gross incomes of those in receipt of more than £1,000 a year,[13] one can be absolutely certain that the £8,000 a year man is not saving £1,600 out of his income today, which he would have to do to maintain the same savings ratio.

We have a system of income tax in which the top rate of tax upon earned income rises to 83 per cent and the top rate of tax upon investment incomes rises to 98 per cent. There are, or there were until we were plunged into yet another economic crisis, proposals to toughen up even this draconian system in some unspecified way. In the debate following the Budget in which he imposed the 98 per cent rate, the Chancellor of the Exchequer, Mr Denis Healey, said these words: 'I believe that this type of redistribution through the tax system makes a major contribution to the health of the community as a whole – and I intend to go a great deal further before I have finished.'

Now I think that, on the contrary, tax rates of this order do a grave disservice to the community. Let me, unlike Mr Healey, give my reasons. The first, which will come as no surprise after my definition of the middle class, is that they make thrift in any meaningful sense impossible. This not merely discourages independence and self-reliance, but it means that a high-taxation society becomes self-perpetuating. From an economic point of view, a pound saved is as 'good' to the Government in terms of regulating consumption and, indeed, of Government finance as a pound taken in taxation. Low savings mean high taxation, high taxation means low savings. One aspect of freedom, though it may be an unfashionable aspect these days, is freedom to choose what to do with one's money, to spend it and save it according to one's own judgement rather than have the Government do all the spending, and very occasionally the saving, on one's behalf.

Second, I believe that it is a positive good, and one that the middle class on the whole sees the virtue of, not to be reliant on the State for everything, or at any rate, for a large part of one's requirements. I believe that society is better, on the whole, if power is as widely dispersed as possible, and that it is not possible to have power dispersed unless wealth is dispersed also. Even the best of people can suffer a subtle form of corruption when they become too dependent on State patronage. When M.P.s discuss their own salaries the debate is rarely edifying; one looks to the Civil Service with their pensions, inflation-proofed since 1971, and their salaries fixed on supposed principles of comparability with outside industry and one sees the creation of a very large vested interest, and one that does not bode very well for the future.

Third, very high taxation on earned income discourages the payment of high salaries. Since so many theorists would regard this as a positive advantage, let me spell out some of its disadvantages to the economy. English executives, finding it impossible to save in their early years (and latterly in their later ones as well) are frozen into immobility. The American system is not perfect, but it does have advantages to the firm and the economy. If an executive has been able to save a fairly substantial sum by his early thirties, he can take the risk of moving to another job, or even of setting up on his own. In this country, by contrast, he has to be very sure of himself before he can consider moving.

Time and again there may be no real financial inducement for him to do so. I even know of cases where the compassionate firm has wanted to fire the less than efficient and has stayed its hand because of the hardship it would cause to an individual without savings. (The reverse of this process is seen in a firm which, being overmanned, decided to offer cash inducements to persuade a percentage of its executives to go. The results were disastrous. Those with ambition and enterprise eagerly took the generous capital sum and went. The firm was left with the dead wood.)

We even have the ludicrous situation where companies are unable to bring their employees back from overseas for substantial promotions at home because there is no way under our tax system to make it worth their while.

One leading multinational company operates a job classification system for all its senior management positions throughout the world, and indeed interchanges executives between its various companies. Thus it can make an accurate comparison between salary levels. Table 3 shows the position for one of its senior managerial posts in October 1974.

TABLE 3

Country	Gross Salary	Net Salary	Difference over U.K. Gross %	Net
U.K.	£15,200	£8,075		
Holland	£30,483	£12,890	+100	+ 60
France	£30,354	£22,118	+100	+174
Germany	£32,254	£18,864	+112	+134
U.S.A.	£31,150	£21,970	+105	+170

The figures speak for themselves. It is not altogether surprising, however much it may go against the grain of the times, that the company comments: 'The future prosperity of this country may depend upon a positive redistribution of income in favour of the country's manufacturing economy. This would appear to be a "fair" result judged by the practice and relative success of comparable national economies.'[14]

Most important of all, in my view, is the fact that steadily decreasing inequality to which the figures bear eloquent testimony has not led to a lessening of envy or discontent. On the contrary, these increase year by year. I suspect that, as the inequality diminishes, the grievances increase. I am sure that we pay a high price in economic distortions as more and more energy at every level from shop floor to boardroom is devoted to getting paid in non-taxable ways. Much more important than any narrowly fiscal distortion is the distortion of viewpoint that concentrates always on the distribution of wealth, never on its creation. Our taxation system is not the sole cause of our poor economic performance, but it is part of it.

These things are, in the nature of things, unquantifiable, but a better economic performance, a faster growth rate, would have benefited the nation as a whole and the mass of the population far more than any measure of redistribution has, or confiscation could. That is why, even on the narrowest view, it is not selfish, and it does not display any want of caring and compassion, to make a call for lower rates of what used to be called 'surtax' and are now, strictly speaking, the higher rates of the unified income-tax system, the first essential in any plan for middle-class survival. The sad – or encouraging – thing is that to reduce the top rate of tax on incomes to 50 per cent would cost no more than £400 million. The net loss would be far smaller, since against this has to be set the loss of revenue from those, ranging from pop stars to distinguished and successful novelists, driven abroad by our tax laws, and the loss of output from those who have no incentive to lift themselves into the higher tax brackets. There is an overwhelming case, too, for the abolition of the surcharge on investment income, which is better regarded as a tax on savings. The old term 'unearned income', used to describe what, in many cases, is the fruit of self-denial, indicates the wealth of prejudice against saving. Oddly enough, the introduction of a negative income tax (which amounts to a guaranteed minimum income for everyone) at the same time could abolish literally 'at a stroke' the poverty which we are assured is still with us in spite of sixty years of redistributive taxation.

4 How inflation hurts

There is a saying of Karl Marx, which has become a cliché in progressive circles, to the effect that the purpose of Marxism is not to understand the world but to change it. The purpose of this book is to help the middle class to change their world. This we can none of us do unless we understand what has been happening to us. In the previous chapter I suggested that the first main enemy of the middle class (and, indirectly, of the nation) was confiscatory tax rates. The purpose of this chapter is to identify an enemy that works hand in hand with the tax system. It is not going too far to say that, until now, the middle class has been merely squeezed. If inflation continues unchecked it will be destroyed.

So far, this may seem to be no more than a platitude. Everyone is against inflation. Every group from the trade unions to the old age pensioners denounces it, and the Government periodically announces dramatic programmes to combat it. In fact, the unanimity of opinion against inflation is even more impressive than the weight of opinion against sin. After all everyone denounces inflation but not everyone denounces sin; indeed quite a number of people announce that they are in favour of specific forms of it, adultery, say, while the more progressive members of the clergy deny that it exists. In fact, there is almost as much hypocrisy about inflation as there is about sin. Both persist because sufficient people find them attractive and apparently beneficial. For long periods in the early stages of an inflation, economists who argue that its effects are wholly damaging are about as likely to be believed as would be a moralist trying to tell a philosophical burglar that robbery is a great evil. The moralist may see that unchecked robbery would lead eventually to a breakdown of society which might not benefit even the burglar.

To the burglar this is hypothetical; what he can see is that it makes him a good deal better off.

If we ask who benefits from inflation – at least in its early stages – the honest answer has to be: most of the population for some of the time, some of the population for most of the time, and the Government all the time. The early stages of an inflation, when money is being gently debased and most people act in the expectation that prices will be stable (i.e. under the illusion that it is not losing its value), can be quite pleasant; economic activity is, or appears to be, stimulated and, indeed, up to around 1970 it was a commonplace for economists to suggest a gentle inflation, a price rise of 1 per cent or 2 per cent a year, as a means of keeping the economy running at a high rate of activity. It is also a means, in the early stages, of squaring the circle, of getting more money without creating more wealth. That is why I said that it benefits most of the population some of the time.

Sooner or later this effect of inflation passes. In this country we are well past that stage; after the early intoxication the hangover is extremely unpleasant. The way in which it benefits some of the population lasts a good deal longer. It causes an arbitrary and unplanned redistribution of wealth. Anyone holding assets in a monetary form is robbed, as holders of War Loan will hardly need to be told. Anyone holding the right sort of non-cash assets, whether it is gold or houses or antique silver, benefits, at least for a time, though even they may find, as many house-owners have done, that in the later stages of an inflation their assets are subject to sudden and unpredictable drops in value. Lenders suffer, borrowers gain as their debt becomes steadily less, provided, that is, that they can keep up with their interest payments. Any groups with the bargaining power to keep their incomes ahead of inflation benefit, though only at the expense of other weaker groups who are left behind, and so this, too, is a form of redistribution: towards the strong, away from the weak.

The way in which it benefits Governments lasts longest of all. To start with, as Professor Milton Friedman has repeatedly pointed out, inflation is a form of taxation, but one that does not have to be legislated for. As paper incomes rise to take account of inflation, the tax takes increases, partly as people at the lower end of the scale are brought into the tax net as their income rises, partly as the better-off are moved into higher and higher tax brackets and partly from almost everyone as the value of allowances is eroded. At the same time, taxes on companies increase as they are taxed on paper profits, and where there are capital gains taxes these are levied on monetary increases in value even when the real value of the asset has fallen. This is a great help to Governments which have an insatiable appetite for revenue; they are enabled to deploy sums of money which would never come their way if they had to be legislated for.

The second way in which inflation helps Governments is that, for a time, it helps them to maintain higher levels of employment than would otherwise be possible. Since all Western Governments have been committed for the past thirty years to the goal of full employment, and since British Governments in particular have believed this to be essential to ensure their return to office, their toleration of inflation is not surprising. However, in anything more than the short to medium term, the benefits inflation brings Governments prove to be as illusory as those it brings other groups. Governments find, as Mr Wilson's Government discovered in the summer of 1975, that because of inflation they have to accept a higher level of unemployment than they ever thought possible. They find, too, that inflation in the long run makes them very unpopular, so that their aim of re-election is not achieved.

All these disadvantages take time to be felt. If I stress the pleasant effects that, in the meantime, seem to follow, if I ask the question *Cui bono?* – Who benefits? – it is because I want to explain the persistence of inflation. It does not persist because nobody knows what to do about it. It persists for one of two reasons. Either its early symptoms are pleasant to too many people, or the pains of inflation are regarded as preferable to the pains of checking it. If you doubt this, you have only to contrast the post-war record of West Germany to that of the United Kingdom. The Germans, with their memories of the hyper-inflation of the 1920s, genuinely detest inflation and have therefore consistently kept it in check. We have not. Even in the past eighteen months, when the whole world has been suffering the effects of the Arab oil crisis, the Germans have kept their inflation rate well down into single figures. In the U.K. it rose to 25 per cent per annum before the Government thought of taking action.

Throughout the recent (and continuing) crisis, it has been suggested that the cause of the inflation we have been suffering is the action of the Arabs at the end of 1974 in quadrupling the price of oil. That this is a nonsense is shown by the contrasting British and German experience. It may be disagreeable to have to spend hundreds of millions of pounds more upon oil, but it is not in itself inflationary unless we continue to buy as much of everything else as before. If the increased spending on oil was balanced by reduced spending on other goods, the effect of the overall level of prices would be very small. The inflation, in other words, came about from a conscious choice, or at any rate, from a constant determination to try to maintain a standard of living when, logically, it ought to have gone down.

That it is false simply to blame the current crisis on the Arabs can, too, be seen from the following table. It shows the percentage rise in retail prices, not just from year to year, but in five-year periods. It shows that a price rise which even in 1965–70 took five years, now takes one year.[15] But it also shows a steady build-up in the rate of inflation over the past twenty years (Table 4).

TABLE 4   Percentage Rise in Retail Prices during Five-year and One-year Periods

Five years		One year	
1955–60	14	1971	2
1960–65	19	1972	7½
1965–70	25	1973	9
1970–75	85	1974	16
1971–76	96	1975	24
		1976	16½

This suggests another important fact about our inflation, that it is progressive, in the sense of tending to increase year by year unless strong measures are taken. If we take a 15 per cent inflation rate, which is after all lower than the going rate for 1974 or

1976, this means that prices double every five years. At this rate they would go up more than 16,000 times during a seventy-year life; that is to say that a £15,000 house would change hands seventy years later for £266 million. One has only to quote these figures or to glance at the table to see how unlikely it is that inflation will continue at this sort of rate. Either it takes off into the realms of hyper-inflation, in which case the currency becomes valueless, and some kind of a new start with a new currency has to be made; or the rate of inflation is slowed right down.

I shall have something to say later about the cost of either process, but first I want to indicate why continuing inflation, even inflation at a good deal less than the 1975 rate, is peculiarly destructive of, and should be peculiarly abhorrent to, the middle class.

It is not merely that the middle class in general finds it extremely hard to maintain its real income and standard of living during rapid inflation. There are two reasons for this. The first is that, as a whole, it lacks the bargaining power of those groups that can, to some extent, protect themselves at the expense of the rest of the community. This is less true than it was as 'white-collar' trade unions begin to ape the militancy of other older-established unions, but, as against this, large sections of the self-employed have no bargaining power at all.

The other reason is the nature of the tax system. After the basic allowances (£1,555 at the beginning of 1977 in the case of a married man with two children under eleven) and items such as allowable mortgage interest, tax is deducted as follows:

First £5,000	35 per cent
£5,001–£5,500	40 per cent
£5,501–£6,500	45 per cent
£6,501–£7,500	50 per cent
£7,501–£8,500	55 per cent
£8,501–£10,000	60 per cent
£10,001–£12,000	65 per cent
£12,001–£15,000	70 per cent
£15,001–£20,000	75 per cent
Above £20,000	83 per cent

This means, of course, that anyone paying income tax at the basic rate needs a percentage increase larger than the increase in the cost of living to keep pace with inflation. The £2,000 a year man (again with two children under eleven) needs a 13 per cent increase to keep pace with 10 per cent inflation. But from £5,800 onwards, a level to which inflation pushes more and more people, the higher rates of tax begin to bite. Progressively, if inflation continues, it becomes impossible for higher-rate tax-payers to maintain their standard of living; the £10,000 a year man who, because of the nominal size of his income, may rarely get an increase as large as the rise in the cost of living, will find he pays 58 per cent of it out in tax.

If, on the other hand, we take inflation at 25 per cent, the level reached in 1975, the picture becomes still more alarming.[16] Table 5 shows the increase in gross income needed to maintain a given net income in real terms for a married man with two children.

TABLE 5

Present income gross	Required income to meet 25 per cent inflation
£	Gross equivalent
2,000	£2,693 (+34%)
4,000	£5,193 (+30%)
6,000	£8,012 (+33%)
8,000	£11,199 (+40%)
10,000	£14,509 (+45%)
15,000	£23,504 (+57%)
20,000	£33,224 (+66%)

But these figures represent merely what needs to be done to meet the inflation of a single year. If the rate of inflation continues year by year, then year by year the process has to be repeated, and year by year it becomes more impossible. The £6,000 a year man has become an £8,000 a year man and thus needs not a 33 per cent increase but one of 40 per cent, and so on.

This is a most powerful element of arbitrary, unplanned re-distribution added to the planned redistribution discussed in the previous chapter. If I describe it as the least important of the

detriments inflation brings the middle classes, this is not to minimize its unpleasantness. It is because the indexation of tax allowances and tax thresholds, for which there should be the loudest
possible agitation, would correct it overnight.

The effect of inflation on savings I regard as far more serious.
It is not so much that, in a frantic scramble to keep pace with the
cost of living, saving becomes a habit harder and harder to
maintain, though this is true. All recent experience indeed shows
that people in general try to increase their savings in a time of
great economic uncertainty. So far from there being a flight out
of money, people, realizing they need a reserve, would rather
save in rapidly depreciating pounds than have nothing at all to
fall back on. But the essence of rational saving is the ability to
plan ahead. What inflation does is to divorce from thrift all order
and system, any hope of sensible planning. It is precisely the
plainer, simpler folk, who have their savings in deposit accounts,
in building societies, in Government securities, who suffer the
worst. In theory, it is possible to choose assets that will rise in line
with inflation. In practice it gets harder and harder, as the kind
of liquidity squeeze that inflation sooner or later brings (paradoxically a shortage of money is one of the symptoms of inflation) is liable to lead to forced selling and bring prices crashing
down.

Those who have put their faith in equity investment as an
inflation hedge since the war have certainly had a rude shock.
The equity index has far outpaced Government securities but
today is lower in real terms than it was before the war. As for the
fall in Stock Exchange values that has taken place since 1972, this
may, in part, be ascribed to the fear (and reality) of socialist
measures, but much of it stems from the manner in which inflation has robbed companies of their cash reserves and meant the
ever-heavier taxing of paper values. As for the sudden doubling
of Stock Exchange values in the early part of 1975 (though still to
a level far below that at which many investors bought in the
previous decade) this is typical of the erratic behaviour of stock
markets in highly inflationary periods.

In the extreme of a hyper-inflation such as the Germans ex-
perienced in the 1920s, money savings virtually vanish. Our own

milder version of inflation, if it continues, besides having a brutal effect on those on non-indexed fixed incomes – non-State retirement pensioners, for example, or those living on a modest nestegg – will prove sufficient to complete the euthanasia of the saving classes.

Nor is this all. Nothing so efficiently weakens the bonds of any society as sustained inflation. Keynes quotes Lenin as saying, 'If you want to destroy capitalism, debauch the currency.' For capitalism you might equally read democracy. Because inflation distributes its apparent rewards and real punishments in so totally arbitrary a fashion, it powerfully reinforces the impulses towards envy, hatred, malice and all uncharitableness that are already painfully evident. Because it is constantly redistributing wealth without rhyme or reason, it focuses even the least malicious mind on the comparison between his position and that of his neighbour. The worst of it is that two great camps open up. One of them contains all the people whose lives have been shaped on the assumption that money is going to remain a reasonably stable store of value. They include private pensioners who discover only a year or two after retirement that the sum that seemed sufficient to give them a modest competence is now totally inadequate, that the house they chose to retire to is now too expensive for them to maintain. To these must be added people with endowment assurance policies which would once have afforded an adequate sum on maturity, but the proceeds of which suddenly seem derisory, and those many people saving through the stock market who see their savings ravaged by an inflationary collapse in Stock Exchange prices.

Behind all these people, directly and immediately affected, hovers an anxious legion – people still working and looking forward to drawing a private pension at some time in the future, who are beginning to realize that there is no way that the managers of their pension funds can obtain the kind of return on their investment needed to keep up with inflation.

They are in the one camp. In the other camp are those public servants fortunate enough to have their pensions linked to the cost of living. This move, which seemed, when it was made in 1971, merely a prudent and sensible step, is now seen to confer on its beneficiaries a status which makes them the object of envy of all the rest. I am not suggesting that they are necessarily protected from inflation in other ways, but the fact is that we suddenly have a division into two nations in a particularly brutal form – those whose benefits are index-linked and those whose benefits are not. Another symptom of these intolerable pressures is white-collar unionism, which may well proceed with a ruthlessness (as the airline pilots have shown) that can more than match that of any organized group of manual workers.

It thus divides the middle class, strikes at all the most vital elements of its existence – thrift, responsibility, forward thinking and stability. It destroys its hope for the future. In the end it undermines the stability of the State, either directly through hyperinflation, or because, if it is left long enough, the measures needed to curb it involve hitherto unacceptable degrees of hardship.

In the end, the metaphor which most closely corresponds to the course of an inflation is that of drug addiction. Small doses seem harmless at first, and the effects surprisingly pleasant. Soon larger and larger doses are needed to produce even the semblance of well-being. If unchecked, it is fatal to the patient but – and this is the dreadful part – the patient violently resists, not so much the notion, but the actuality of cure, since the withdrawal symptoms are so agonizing. In the end, a time may come when the patient has to be coerced and that is the death, perhaps not of the patient, but of democracy.

I have depicted the matter in these terms, which do not overstate the case, quite simply to warn the middle class that, of all their enemies, inflation is the chief. Unless and until there is an end to that kind of complicity between Government and governed which leads to the maximum promise of action against inflation combined with the minimum being effectively done, it is wholly idle for them to seek to arrest their decline. The theme has been the effects rather than the mechanism of inflation. But it is hardly possible to pass over in complete silence the economics of the subject. It is not possible to mobilize anyone to demand a cure unless they have some idea of the nature of the disease and of what is involved in checking it. The rest of this chapter, therefore, seeks to give answers, in as basic a form as possible, to three key questions: what is inflation, what is the relationship between inflation and unemployment, and how can inflation be checked? Those with professional knowledge of these topics can hurry on; it is not designed for them.

Nine people out of ten, if asked what inflation is, will reply in terms of rising prices, everything getting dearer in the shops. The first thing to say, therefore, is that rising prices are a symptom not a cause of inflation. In any relatively free system, prices are constantly changing relative to one another, and even in a time of inflation some things become cheaper; refrigerators, for example, dropped dramatically in price between the forties and the sixties. Equally, it is quite possible for some prices to go up dramatically without this being inflationary. When the Arabs, for example, quadrupled the price of oil, this was highly inconvenient, but if we had simply bought less of other things it would have had little or no inflationary effect at all. Indeed (and this illustrates why the man in the street is so liable to become confused on these topics) the oil price rise was in itself deflationary, in the sense that it led to a reduction in purchasing power available for other goods and services and so to a slow-down in world trade and a resultant drop in commodity prices. What was highly inflationary was the reaction to the oil price rise. Governments – or at any rate, the British Government – pretended that one could pay the increased price for oil *and* go on consuming as much of everything else as before. In other words, they went on printing money to help meet the extra costs.

This leads to the central point – that inflation is essentially a relationship between the volume of money in circulation and the volume of goods available. When the amount of money rises – or falls – in step with the production and availability of goods, there is no inflation and the price level is stable. (Availability is as important as production. In wartime, for example, shells are produced and promptly exploded, but the money paid for them circulates and leads, unless special measures are taken, to inflation.)

Inflation then is best regarded as a debasement in the value of money and few things are more important than to keep this simple fact in mind. We are often told that wage claims are inflationary.

This is true only insofar as more money is made available to finance successful wage claims and the subsequent rise in prices. To some, the distinction may seem like hair-splitting if the power of the trade unions is such as to persuade Governments that they have no option but to make the money available. Even in the public sector, however, where the Government is the direct employer, the largest pay claim would not be inflationary if the Government resolved to put an absolute ceiling on its total wage bill, a policy towards which it is beginning cautiously to move.

Such a policy means, of course, that higher pay would result simply in fewer jobs being available and this leads directly to the second question, the relationship between inflation and unemployment. Put at its simplest, one principal reason why Governments of all parties have been prepared to print money far over and above any increase in production, is that they have shared a commitment to maintaining full employment and, since the war, have given it the highest priority of any single domestic policy. There is no doubt either that, in so doing, they have been acting in accord with public opinion. The memories of the 1930s, when unemployment was never less than 10 per cent, were etched in the minds of Conservative as well as Socialist politicians, and, indeed, in those of the general public. When unemployment rose, they believed that it was up to the Government to give a boost to demand, if need be, by pumping out money. The classic case of this was the reaction of the Conservative Government in 1972, when the unemployment figure reached one million. It was as though an alarm bell had sounded. The then Chancellor of the Exchequer, Mr Barber, expanded credit to an unprecedented degree. This did bring unemployment down for a time, but it had other consequences too. It led to the boom in house prices and property speculation which was such a feature of 1972–3; it also led to the quite unprecedented rate of inflation in 1974 and 1975.

The attempt to ensure full employment simply by manipulating demand has indeed two large drawbacks. The first of these is that, when demand is increased too far and too fast, imports are sucked in and we have one of Britain's periodic balance of payments crises. Sooner or later, this has to be corrected, which leads to a cutback in home demand and rising unemployment – all the symptoms of 'stop'. Then, when the balance of payments is looking healthier, unemployment becomes the main issue again – and so demand is stepped up, inflationary finance recommences and off we go on the next phase of the stop–go cycle so familiar to everyone since the war.

The second disadvantage is much more grave. Post-war experience shows that the use of the technique of pumping money out becomes less and less effective each time it is used. What happens is that both inflation and unemployment become steadily worse. At the peak of the boom when the economy shows every sign of overheating and the balance of payments is deteriorating fast, unemployment is higher than at the peak of the previous boom. At the bottom of the trough when output is stagnating and unemployment felt to be very high, inflation is still running at a level higher than in the last recession.

There are good, though unpalatable, reasons why this should be so. In a nutshell (and these are matters that deserve a book to themselves) what has been called the 'natural' level of unemployment is dictated by a number of real factors – how productive industry is, how easy or difficult it is for people to be retrained or moved from one job to another, or one area of the country to another, and so on. It is possible, for a short time, to push down unemployment by pumping out money but the price of each artificial boost is an accelerating rate of inflation. What is more, at each stage in the process the rate of inflation relative to any given level of unemployment below the 'natural' rate is higher than before.

That is why we are no longer, if we ever were, in the happy position of deciding it is worth putting up with a little more inflation if this means a lot less unemployment. The time finally comes, as we have seen in Britain over the past eighteen months, when the inflation itself leads to unemployment, as companies run out of cash.

Then, if and when the inflation becomes intolerable and steps are taken to check it, we begin to see just how many people have been kept in particular jobs only by the rising level of inflation. Equally unpleasant, as the inflation is wrung out of the system, there is a temporary fall in business activity and a temporary rise in unemployment above the 'natural' level. That is one reason why curing inflation is extremely unpleasant. Another is that it involves an end to the world of illusion in which there seems to be no link between how much we produce and how much we pay ourselves. To say all this is not to deny that unemployment is a grave evil or that it is an important task of Governments to reduce it; only that the way to deal with unemployment is to attack its real causes and not to enter the shadow world of inflation.

What, then, is the cure for inflation? It is not enough to say, though formally speaking it is true, that inflation is a monetary phenomenon and must be dealt with by monetary means. An end to recurrent artificial attempts to stimulate the economy; a determination gradually to slow down the increase in the money supply and, thereafter, allow only a steady, unsensational increase in the money supply year by year; elimination of the budget deficit; a cut in the proportion of the national income the State spends; a reduction in taxes on efficiency, effort and thrift. All these things are steps along the road, but it is vain to suggest that, however patiently applied, the remedy can be less than distressing. Governments have failed to do these things in the past, not only because they lacked understanding, but because they thought they were 'politically impossible'.

If they remain politically impossible, then there is certainly no hope for the middle class in this country, and probably not much for democracy. Fortunately the boundaries between the possible and the impossible change all the time, as we can observe by watching the actions of the present Government. If the most important single need of the middle class is to realize just what uncontrolled inflation will do to all classes of society, its most important task is to impress on Governments how intolerable this prospect is. The necessary monetary remedies will not be applied until it is clear that informed opinion demands them. It is up to the middle class to show the way.

One final point about the cost of living. I mentioned the gulf opening between those who enjoy cost-of-living indexed benefits and those who do not. There is a strong argument in favour of extending the principle of indexation, to savings, taxes and benefits generally. It will not remove but it will ease the pain of ending inflation; it can make the cure much more tolerable. Great care has, however, to be exercised in its introduction since wrongly applied, without a proper anti-inflationary programme, it can actually speed up the rate of inflation as Mr Heath's cost-of-living 'threshold' payments undoubtedly did. This is an argument, however, for sensible indexation, not for opposing indexation.

Inflation on its own is bad enough; £15,000 net in April 1974 is worth no more (after some 30 per cent inflation) than £11,500 at the end of 1975. Three more years of only 10 per cent per annum inflation and it will be worth less than £8,300. That is the reality of inflation. Inflation plus the present tax system imposes profound changes, changes that the electorate has not willed or voted for. From this point of view indexation is an emergency measure. Without it there will be no time even to think in what direction we wish society to go.

It hardly needs saying that the case for indexing taxes on wealth is at least as strong as for indexing taxes on income. One of the least just and most cruel of all imposts in an inflationary age is to charge Capital Gains Tax upon paper profits caused simply by inflationary rises in value, when, in real terms, the assets have fallen in value. Most of us still under-estimate the devastating effect of inflation on the value of our assets. For that reason I show in Charts 1 and 2 the *Financial Times* Ordinary Share Index and the price of War Loan, both in money terms and with their values adjusted for the cost of living. They are well worth pondering upon. They show that £100 invested in shares in 1935 was worth £50 in real terms at the end of 1975. £100 invested in War Loan in the same year was worth £2·70 at the end of 1975. That is the reality of saving in an age of inflation.

1   The Effect of Inflation

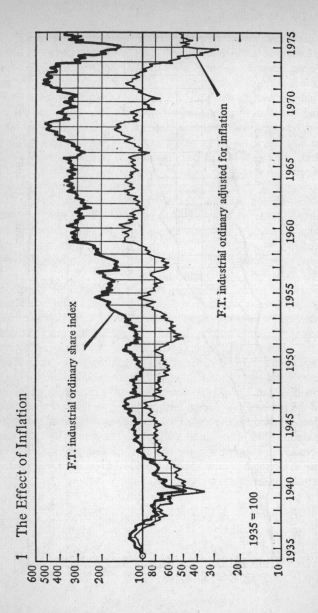

F.T. industrial ordinary share index

F.T. industrial ordinary adjusted for inflation

1935 = 100

2 Forty Years of War Loan

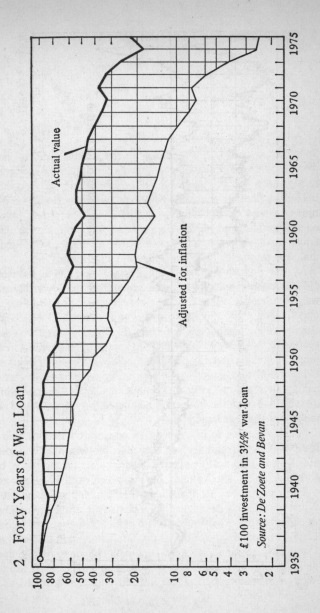

Actual value

Adjusted for inflation

£100 investment in 3½% war loan

Source: De Zoete and Bevan

5 Mr Heath and Mr Healey

So far, in discussing the pressures on the middle class, we have discussed the general pattern of redistribution over the years, seen how far redistribution has really gone, and identified inflation as the most powerful single engine of destruction. It is now time to have a closer look at the years 1970–75 and their impact on the middle class. This was the time when the strains, long latent, really began to show, and when for the first time many middle-class people began to despair of their future.

At first sight this is surprising. From June 1970 to February 1974 a Conservative Government, headed by Mr Edward Heath, was in office. It was a Government that was described by its opponents as 'the most reactionary in history' and which was claimed to have indulged in 'massive handouts to the rich'. And yet during this period middle-class people seem to have felt themselves far from cosseted, and by the General Election of February 1974 their dissatisfaction took the traditional forms of abstention and a switch of support to the Liberals. It seems well worthwhile, therefore, to trace the Budgetary history of the years 1970–75 and to see just what occurred.

Mr Heath came to power with an unexpected election win in June 1970. His first choice as Chancellor, Mr Iain Macleod, died suddenly and tragically only a few weeks after taking office, but his replacement, Mr Anthony Barber, was a man of energy and vigour, enjoying the confidence of Mr Heath, and someone determined to make his impact upon the British taxation system. Over his period of office he simplified and unified the system of income tax and surtax, changed the Corporation Tax system under which companies are taxed, reduced modestly the rates of tax upon higher incomes, abolished Purchase Tax and the unpopular Selective Employment Tax and introduced Value Added Tax in their place. He also planned to combine large parts of the personal tax allowance system and the social services benefits into a single system of tax credits. This would have been of very considerable help to the lower paid, many of whom, under the present system, do not earn enough to benefit fully from their personal tax allowances, and/or do not fully take up the social security benefits to which they are entitled. Unfortunately, Mr Barber was not in office long enough to get this last scheme beyond the discussion stage, and despite his hopes that it might prove to be a bipartisan policy, it seemed, following the return of the Labour Party to office in 1974, to have sunk without trace, and only now is Conservative interest in it beginning to revive.

As far as positive tax reductions are concerned, one of Mr Barber's early actions, in October 1970, was to announce that the standard rate of income tax was to be reduced from 41·25 per cent to 38·75 per cent with effect from 6 April 1971. There is no doubt that the reaction to this 6d. cut was deeply disappointing to the Government. It was combined with some expenditure cuts, some of which proved highly unpopular, notably the decision to end general free school milk (which, in spite of the brouhaha at the time, has never been reversed). The Government seemed to have expected that what was, after all, a very minor measure of tax reduction would have had an instantaneous and electrifying effect – Mr Heath, who coined the phrase 'instant Government' to describe Mr Wilson's style of ruling, himself seemed constantly to expect immediate results from anything that he did. The March 1971 Budget increased income tax child allowances and also earned-income relief for all earned income over £4,005. In March 1972 the married and single allowances were increased by £135, but this, in fairness, was little more than one of the steps periodically taken to remove from the taxation net some of those that inflation is constantly bringing in at the bottom of the scale.

Apart from cuts in the level of indirect taxation, which were of benefit to all, Mr Barber did three things which could be taken as giving specific help to the middle classes. He arranged for the repayment of all outstanding post-war credits (by now, alas, sadly depleted in real value) by December 1973. He eased the pressure of estate duty a little, in particular providing for an exemption of up to £15,000 left to the surviving spouse. Above all, when he unified the tax system, bringing together income tax and surtax, the new combined scale collected some £250 millions less than would have been paid under the old system. This compares with overall reductions in the total amount of income tax levied through the increases in personal allowances and so on of nearly £1,800 million, but it was the basis of the charge that there had been 'massive handouts to the rich' and, indeed, speakers at successive Labour Party conferences did not scruple to add a convenient nought on to the figure and make it £2,500 millions. This left the top rate of tax on earned income at 75 per cent and on investment income at 90 per cent.

But what was the net impact of these various reliefs on the position of the middle class? The best calculation was made by *The Economist*[17] which demonstrated that in practice Mr Barber balanced the buoyancy of the revenue (higher money incomes, higher tax, leaving one worse off in real terms) almost exactly by his tax cuts. Strangely enough, these produced almost precisely the same effect as if he had indexed tax scales in the way I suggested in the last chapter. For example, a senior executive earning £10,000 a year would have needed £30,000 a year by 1973 just to maintain the same standard of living after the 43 per cent 1968–73 price rise, if taxes had stayed where they were in 1968. Thanks to the Barber tax cuts, however, he needed only a 49 per cent rise – very close to the inflation rate – to stay where he was. Table 6 shows how this works for other incomes.

TABLE 6   Percentage Increase Needed to 1973 to Preserve Real After-tax Income

1968 income	At 1968 tax rates and allowances	At 1973 tax rates and allowances
£ p.a.	(%)	(%)
1,000	53	48
2,000	48	47
5,000	60	44
7,500	93	47
10,000	199	49
15,000	221	33

Above £10,000 a year, as the impact of the concessions increases, the percentage increase required lessens, but at these levels the increases, too, tend to be less, so that the overall relationship very largely holds.

The net effect then of the Barber tax reductions on earned income was to neutralize for a period the pain of inflation, at least to those who received the average increase. Of course, there are in the middle classes a great many people, particularly those in the self-employed category, who are not in a position to award themselves pay increases commensurate with inflation, and they will have continued to suffer in the usual way.

As far as investment income is concerned, Mr Barber's concessions had a nominally more substantial effect if only because the tax rates on so-called unearned income were so heavy. For example, a married couple earning £6,000 a year found their effective tax rate reduced from 28·1 per cent to 26·5 per cent between 1971 and 1973. If their £6,000 a year had all been investment income, their effective rate of tax would have come down from 48·2 per cent to 36·5 per cent. On the other hand, it is very doubtful if investment incomes could be expected to rise in line with the cost of living in the way that many salaries did and so, in real terms, the benefit, if any, would be very much diminished.

Here, we may note two irritations caused by the Barber tax reforms. Many small businesses found the introduction of Value Added Tax, which made every shopkeeper, every businessman and every professional man in the land (provided that their turnover amounted to £5,000 a year or more) an unpaid tax collector, a complete nightmare. This is inherent in the V.A.T. system to which we were committed by the decision to join the Common Market, and incredible though it may seem the British system is simpler by far than that obtaining in most other countries. Second, the new unified tax system meant that tax at the higher rates had to be paid on the pay-as-you-earn system instead of a year in arrears as under the old surtax system. There was therefore one dreadful year in which two years' surtax was payable, and even a concession which enabled it to be paid on deferred terms scarcely lessened the price that had to be paid for the change.

Nonetheless, we can say of Mr Barber's time at the Treasury

that it was benevolent in intention and that, if his fiscal policy did little to restore the position of the middle class, it did nothing to erode it. The same, unfortunately, cannot be said of the Heath Government's 'anti-inflation' policy. Had one not seen Mr Wilson introduce the Social Contract and lived to see its totally predictable and totally predicted failure, one would have said that no policy to deal with inflation could have been more misconceived than that of Mr Heath. Alarmed, as I said in the last chapter, by an unemployment figure that had risen to one million, the Government in 1972 swung the economy from 'stop' into 'go' by means of measures including a very large expansion of Government spending, a very large expansion of credit and a truly massive expansion of the money supply. Having instituted these inflationary measures, it then attempted to tie the lid down on the kettle with a variety of incomes policies – Stage One, Stage Two and Stage Three. Because Stage Three ended with a confrontation with the coal-miners, the calling of a General Election and the effective defeat of the Heath Government, it is easy to forget that what characterized all the earlier stages was a desperate search for agreement with the trade unions. Long, weary hours were spent in negotiations with the T.U.C. General Council, and though Mr Heath did not, in the event, succeed in getting its agreement, he did everything possible to ensure its acquiescence. This was a period rich in ironies. The confrontation with the miners arose out of Stage Three, which had been tailor-made on the advice of Mr Joe Gormley, the miners' leader, to enable the Coal Board to offer terms it was thought that the Executive of the National Union of Mineworkers could accept. The Prime Minister was labelled as 'abrasive' when most of his time was spent on a search for consensus; his Government was labelled 'right-wing' when the ideal he consistently pursued, that of 'fairness', and his desire to do a deal with the unions meant that he ruthlessly disregarded the interests of the middle class during the successive phases of his incomes policy.

To give the most obvious example, the permitted increases under Phase Three ranged from 7 per cent at the lower levels to only £350 a year or $3\frac{1}{2}$ per cent at £10,000 a year. The effect of this was to ensure, for all Mr Barber's tax reforms, that anyone paying tax at more than the standard rate would not hope to keep pace with inflation and would suffer a drop in their standard of living from 1974 on. Equally, dividend limitation hit hard at those dependent on the income from their savings, while price controls, though superficially popular, helped with disastrous effect to undermine the profitability of industry. The self-employed, of course, were often simply not in the position to grant themselves increases. The middle class has to realize, in fact, that whoever else may gain from an incomes policy, *it* will always be the loser. There are three reasons for this. First, the restraints imposed with an allegedly impartial hand press more heavily on a largely un-organized section of the community than on the more powerful trade unions. Second, to gain the assent of the T.U.C. as Mr Wilson and Mr Callaghan did, or to attempt to gain it as Mr Heath did, involves always and inevitably spiteful measures against the better-off. Third, the distortions that Pay Boards and Price Commissions impose on the economy, and the bureau-cratization of society that they involve, inevitably militate against the energetic and the enterprising. One can argue, in addition, that society as a whole is a net loser from such attempts. Con-centration upon an incomes policy distracts attention from what needs to be done; it may indeed worsen inflation insofar as the ceiling imposed on wages becomes a floor, and it encourages Governments to think 'it is safe to reflate' – with disastrous results.

Be that as it may, many middle-class people must have won-dered by the beginning of 1974 why, after three and a half years of Conservative Government, they felt no better than they did. The brief answer is that, though the Barber tax measures helped them not to slip back further, the general policies of the Heath Government both worsened their relative position and helped to weaken the whole middle-class ethos. Moreover, it was this Government that, from 1972 on, unleashed the hound of infla-tion through its over-expansion of credit.

King Log is, perhaps, too kind a description of Mr Heath's attitudes to the middle class. In a revealing message to the Young Conservatives at their annual conference at Eastbourne after he had been deposed by the Parliamentary Conservative Party, he spoke of always having 'a vision of a Britain where barriers of class and privilege have been shattered, the vision of a society that was just'. He never defined the barriers of class and privilege that he dreamt of shattering and, of course, the rhetoric is preposterous. After the experience of his premiership, the middle class may have felt both shattered and underprivileged. But if he was at best King Log, there is no doubt that, as far as the middle class is concerned, Mr Denis Healey has been, since March 1974, King Stork. (I say Mr Healey rather than Mr Wilson or Mr Callaghan because of the big differences in their styles of government. There never was any doubt that it was a Heath Government, with the imprint of his personality on all its actions and activities. Mr Wilson, on the other hand, presides over a team that often seems to be riding off in all directions. Moreover there is a particular brutality about Mr Healey and his approach to Budgetary matters that is uniquely his own.)

At the last Labour Party Conference before the February 1974 election, Mr Healey had promised that there would be 'howls of anguish from the rich' as a result of his Budget measures. The term 'rich' as we have seen is relative, but he did his best to live up, or down, to his words. In his first Budget, in March 1974, he faced the need to raise £700 millions to increase food and housing subsidies. This he found, in the only way he could, by increasing indirect taxes, and thus putting everyone's cost of living up. He increased the basic rate of income tax from 30 to 33 per cent but raised the tax thresholds slightly, so that the higher tax would begin to bite, for married couples at above £1,800 a year. He then announced another £500 millions of income-tax increases, increasing the top rate of tax on earned incomes from 75 to 83 per cent and on investment incomes to 98 per cent, lowering the starting point for the higher rate of taxes to £4,500 instead of £5,000. He also, which was particularly mean, lowered the starting point for the surcharge on investment income from £2,000 to £1,000, though subsequently, after a long Parliamentary battle, the threshold was temporarily raised to £2,000. The really nasty thing about this particular set of measures is that they amounted to something close to a capital levy. The Treasury, in its calculations, did not expect them to reduce the amount the nation spent

– in other words they would come out of savings not of spending. He also raised retirement pensions, but it must not be thought that his tax measures paid for this socially desirable increase. The cost of his pensions increases was to be covered largely by a rise in the employers' flat-rate insurance contributions. This, one may remark in passing, merely reflected another long-standing socialist delusion, that it is possible to increase social benefits painlessly, by making companies pay.

It is not my purpose to chart the disastrous course of Mr Healey's three 1974 Budgets, except insofar as they hit the middle class. Clearly the February Budget increased their tax just when their standard of living was suffering a fall in any case. A still worse result was that they had the effect of making inflation far worse than it might otherwise have been. Part of this was deliberate, part accidental. There is no doubt that the minority Government formed in February 1974 knew it would have to face another election within the year. It put itself in a position to do so by pumping money out to maintain consumer spending at all costs, at a time when other countries were recognizing that they had to cut back to meet the increased cost of oil. That was the deliberate part. The more accidental way in which inflation was increased was by a vast increase in public spending, some planned, some unplanned, amounting to an 8 per cent increase in real terms, financed entirely by borrowing. By July Mr Healey was cutting the rate of V.A.T. from 10 to 8 per cent (good for consumers) but by this time companies were being starved of cash (and stock market values were plummeting) as a direct result of increases in their taxation in the March Budget.

By November the results were too disastrous even for Mr Healey to contemplate for long and, in any case, the October election had been won. The main point of his autumn Budget was to restore to companies via Corporation Tax relief the money of which they had been mulcted earlier in the year. A Capital Transfer Tax was introduced to replace the old estate duty, and by way of the genuine Healey touch he brought the threshold for investment income down again. The surcharge was to start at £1,000 and to rise from 10 to 15 per cent at the £2,000 level.

There was, however, a concession to the over-sixty-fives; their investment-incomes surcharge did not begin till the £1,500 level. In fairness, however, there was one other important concession to the over-sixty-fives, or at any rate those whose incomes did not exceed £3,840 a year, in the form of an increase in their allowances against tax.

It must not be thought that the Chancellor had abandoned his more general and ferocious ambitions, however. Explaining why his November Budget was not beastlier than it was, he remarked:

The main instrument for achieving the necessary redistribution of wealth and income is our system of personal taxation. I do not intend to introduce legislation this autumn to deal with these issues; the time for dealing with them will be in my spring Budget.

When the spring came, however, the immediate crisis had overtaken Mr Healey's longer-term socialist aims. The borrowing requirement was up from £7,500 millions to £9,000 millions and our overseas creditors were getting restless. On this occasion, the Chancellor had to soak everybody: £625 millions was taken off smokers and drinkers, £270 millions gathered in by increasing vehicle licences, while V.A.T. was raised to 25 per cent on so-called luxuries, including such latter-day essentials as having the washing-machine serviced. (Such was the disastrous effect of the 25 per cent rate that in his April 1976 Budget the 'luxury' rate was halved to 12½ per cent.) The main direct additional middle-class burden was yet another increase, of 2p in the income tax rate, making the standard rate 35 per cent. The top rates, however, remained unchanged at 83 and 98 per cent.

I cannot pretend that the fiscal history of the past five years makes very pleasant reading, but we so quickly forget what has been done to us that it is worth running over the details. The really depressing thing is that, at the end of the five years, not just the position of the middle class, but the position of the nation is so much worse than it was. I shall be dealing with Mr Healey's Capital Transfer Tax and his proposals for a Wealth Tax later in this book. As far as the difference between Mr Barber and Mr Healey is concerned, it is fair to sum up the difference in this way:

Mr Barber intended to help the middle class, Mr Healey set out cold-bloodedly to harm it. But while Mr Barber was Chancellor, the rapid inflation started that Mr Healey has done so much to worsen.

6 The onslaught on the self-employed

Till now we have been concerned with identifying the twin scourges of taxation and inflation as the main *direct* enemies of the middle class. To attack inflation is non-controversial. To attack taxation, however, will at once raise cries of 'selfishness' and accusations of narrowness of vision. Let me emphasize, therefore, that the issue of taxation is central to middle-class survival (and, in the opinion of many, to the survival of a free society). Thrift can only be exercised, choice is only possible, when the individual is left with sufficient of his income to make these meaningful. It is not for the highwayman to complain that his victim is showing an excessive preoccupation with worldly goods.

In this chapter I wish to discuss the prospects of one great segment of the middle class – the self-employed. But before doing so let me point out one way in which both taxation and inflation are bound together to produce a still stronger rope. The level of public expenditure is obviously of immediate middle-class concern; taxation feeds it, and inflation causes it, apparently inexorably, to rise. It is not possible to be interested in taxation and inflation and not concerned with public expenditure. Table 7 gives the picture with startling clarity.[18]

There are three important points that the figures in the table illustrate. The first is a remorseless secular rise over the past hundred years in the proportion of the national income that is disposed of, not by individuals but by Government, central and local. It would be silly to pretend that this is all evil. No one in their right minds would wish to return to the level of social provision of the year 1870. It is equally impossible to doubt that, at some point, the process went too far.

The second point is brought out by the more detailed figures

TABLE 7   Growth in Public Expenditure

Year	Gross National Product £ millions	Total Government expenditure £ millions	As proportion of G.N.P. per cent
1870	990	95	9
1900	1,940	280	14
1920	6,070	1,590	26
1928	4,520	1,095	24
1938	5,290	1,585	30
1950	11,740	4,540	39
1955	16,980	6,145	36
1960	22,820	8,955	39
1965	31,340	14,142	45
1966	33,526	15,318	46
1967	35,535	17,530	49
1968	37,810	19,113	51
1969	39,885	19,796	50
1970	43,809	21,880	50
1971	49,298	24,370	49
1972	55,259	27,407	50
1973	64,321	32,153	50
1974	73,997	41,606	56
1975	94,000	55,200	59

given in the second half of the table for the past decade. They show a rise during two periods of Labour Government 1964–70 and 1974–? but they do not show a fall during the period of Conservative Government in 1970–73. This is another piece of empirical evidence confirming the view that the period of the Heath Government marked at very best a standstill or slowing-down in the decline of the middle class, not a relative improvement.

The third point is one made, strangely enough by Mr Denis Healey at the Labour Party Conference in October 1975. Resisting demands for still more taxation upon 'the rich', he pointed out that the burden of taxation was now weighing upon the whole pupulation to a point at which even he was apparently prepared to consider crying 'Halt'.

'In 1955', the Chancellor told his Blackpool audience, 'an average family with two kids' (children are always kids if it is a Labour audience you are addressing) 'did not start paying income tax at 33 per cent until it was on one and two-thirds average earnings. Today, the average family with two kids is paying 35 per cent when it is only on half average earnings.

'In 1955', he continued, 'a family on average earnings paid only 16 per cent of its income in tax. Now it pays nearly twice as much in tax, 29 per cent, and if we wanted to go on with our existing programmes of public expenditure, then any increase in earnings which you get in 1980, half of that will go in tax and contribution.'

He did not add, which he might have done, that grotesque increases in public spending of the order shown in the table – 8 per cent in real terms and 31·2 per cent in money terms in 1974/5 – imply also a much heavier rates burden, but we are making progress when a Labour Chancellor gets as far as admitting what he did.

Not altogether surprisingly, these leaps in public spending have brought their own nemesis. Throughout 1976 the Government was in very considerable difficulties over its spending programmes. In February 1976 it announced 'cuts' that in fact amounted to a scaling down of future spending programmes. Public spending would continue to rise, though at a slower rate than before. In July, faced with a renewed crisis, it announced further cuts amounting to £1,000 millions. In December, in order to qualify for a loan from the International Monetary Fund, it promised cuts amounting to a further £1,000 millions in 1977/8 and to £1,500 millions in 1978/9. These two sets of cuts were certainly in part more genuine than the February ones, but they fell overwhelmingly upon capital spending programmes, not the Government's current spending. Moreover, as the Government had greatly overestimated the rate at which output would rise, cuts would have been needed merely to stop the percentage of public expenditure rising still further.

In this extremity, the Treasury came to the rescue. Its statisticians re-defined public spending in a way that smartly dropped the 1975 total, for example, from 60 to 52 per cent by excluding various items. But even the new figures show the same sharp rise.

My thesis has been that a burden that bears upon all is peculiarly crippling as far as the aspirations of the middle class are concerned. But there is one section of the middle class that deserves singling out for specific attention from this point of view: the self-employed. They are, after all, by definition people in business on their own account, and as such they are particularly vulnerable to a climate in which a larger and larger proportion of the national income is spent by the State.

Were this all, it might be bad enough, but the combined effect, the totality of Government action over the past twelve years, has been sufficiently crushing to justify the title of this chapter. There has indeed been an onslaught on the self-employed.

I think we have to start with the fact, for which there is abundant empirical evidence, that the Labour Party has very little time for this section of the population. There are, I believe, three strands that can be disentangled in the socialist attitude. The first is very much a trade union attitude, a dislike for those who are individualistic, unorganized, members of no union, seeking their salvation through individual rather than collective action.

The second is a belief that the self-employed represent some uniquely privileged group, and probably one exploiting tax loopholes to the full. The minute base fact on which this prejudice is erected is the fact that, under our taxation system, a Schedule D occupation is more favourably treated than one under Schedule E. The average self-employed person, with no guaranteed employment, no pension beyond what he provides for himself, no holiday pay, no sickness benefit – indeed the knowledge that a prolonged illness may be the end of his business – and the freedom to work unlimited hours, such a person may have a hard time in recognizing himself as privileged. As far as he is concerned, his privilege is to take the risk of bankruptcy. There is one sense, of course, in which he does have a unique privilege. He has the right to be his own master, and it may be that it is the freedom that is so uniquely offensive to socialist nostrils. Be that as it may, he is living in a fool's paradise if he does not recognize his unpopularity.

The third reason why the Labour Party has little time for the self-employed is that, if it has a basic belief, it is in the virtues of monopoly. Ideally it favours State monopolies, but if it is not possible for these to be the only forms of industrial organization, then a Labour Government is at its easiest in dealing with the very largest firms in the country. It can talk easily to the Board of I.C.I. A multiplicity of small firms it finds disturbing.

I have started by stressing this ideological divide because it goes a long way towards explaining the singular want of sympathy towards the self-employed and those concerned with smaller businesses. If I date the onslaught back a dozen years, it is to take us back to Mr Wilson's first administration in 1964 and Mr James Callaghan's Chancellorship. (To those readers not primarily interested in fiscal matters it may seem that there is no escape from the discussion of tax changes. The truth is that, in the modern State, it is primarily through the operation of the tax system, far more than through direct controls, that Governments give or take, bless or curse.)

I happened at this time to be giving financial advice to a modest company, built up through the enterprise of one woman, and I was thus able to experience at first hand the harassment to which it was increasingly subject. I started with the attitude that for someone to give employment to forty or so people was a rather fine and worthwhile thing to do. I soon became aware that this was not the attitude of the Government. Some of the measures enacted by Mr Callaghan in 1965 were trivial in themselves, some were more fundamental, but they all had the effect of increasing the pressure upon small businesses and the self-employed. As an example of the trivial one can instance the disallowance of entertainment expenses for tax purposes, except where an overseas buyer is involved. This can be – and was – represented as a measure to prevent bloated businessmen stuffing themselves in luxurious West End restaurants at the taxpayers' expense. Its practical effect was to bear down very unfairly on a large number of the self-employed whose only opportunity of meeting prospective clients was to take them out to lunch.

As for major legislation with a highly adverse effect, one can instance the introduction of the Corporation Tax system, and in particular Mr Callaghan's 'close company' legislation. Again, the ostensible purpose of bringing in Corporation Tax was to separate the systems of personal and company taxation. Its practical effect was to facilitate using the business sector as a milch cow. Individuals notice when their tax goes up, and have votes, though the evidence in this book suggests that they have not so far been able to use them effectively. But rather than raise general levels of taxation, successive Governments have found it easier to put up company tax. These appear to cost the general public nothing, though in fact nothing is for nothing, and the public soon pay indirectly, with higher prices and less efficient businesses.

Corporation Tax, then, was to raise the level of taxation upon businesses large and small. It also made it much harder to run a business as a limited company. Retained profits were taxed at rates that were never lower than 40 per cent so that it became progressively harder to build up a business from scratch. Dividends, if paid out, were taxed on top of this. However, the rates of Corporation Tax, whether 40 per cent or 50 per cent, were still lower than those levied upon private individuals. At this point the characteristic obsessions of the Labour Party and the Inland Revenue met and corresponded entirely. Both fear, above all else, tax avoidance, and never pause to ask themselves whether a taxation system might be constructed that ordinary, rational people might be less eager to avoid. The introduction of Corporation Tax 'necessitated' the definition of an elaborate system of 'close companies', these being broadly defined as companies under the control of five or fewer persons. Such companies were compelled to distribute nearly all of their investment incomes and at least 60 per cent of their trading profits after tax unless they could convince the Revenue that the money was needed for business purposes. All this led to work, worry, complications and difficulty for those running such a business. It meant, for example, that they had to avoid at all costs showing cash in the balance sheet, however artificial the expedients for achieving this aim. This would give rise to absurdities; it was, for example, inadvisable to make a direct loan to a company one controlled when starting business, as this might show one was flush with cash. Better by far to guarantee a bank loan, and so on.

By these means, trading as a company was made unattractive to many small businesses, while the personal rates of tax made it very hard to build a business up while trading as an individual. One extreme example may suffice. It is conventional to deplore the decline in Stock Exchange jobbing firms – jobbers being in effect wholesalers in shares, ensuring a ready market by making them available to brokers. But until very recently the only partners in jobbing firms were individuals, liable, like all members of the Stock Exchange, to the uttermost farthing of their possessions in case of failure. A jobber can – and could – make very large profits in a good year, but the taxation on these as personal income meant that there was no possibility of building up the kind of reserves needed to preserve the system through more mixed and inflationary times. The result has been a drastic reduction in the numbers of jobbers – and less good service to the public.

Corporation Tax thus became a grievous burden on the smaller businesses, and in particular family ones. But the tax which seems to have caused the greatest protest from the largest number is Valued Added Tax, introduced by Mr Barber and operational from 1973. The reason can be summed up in two sentences. Purchase Tax was levied at 75,000 points. Valued Added Tax was collected from no less than 1,300,000 companies and individuals. This meant that many small businesses found themselves in direct contact with and, in their view, harassed by the Customs and Excise, who are responsible for the collection of the tax, who are used to dealing with smugglers and whose methods are felt by many to be blunt, even compared with those of the Inland Revenue. Employers had long acted as unpaid tax collectors in remitting P.A.Y.E. to the Revenue. Now hundreds of thousands of individuals found themselves enmeshed in the complicated procedures of Value Added Tax on behalf of the Customs and Excise. An additional cause for complaint was the unindexed level of £5,000 at which the liability to register for Value Added Tax was fixed. A great many small, professional men found themselves faced with a dilemma. Either they kept their total receipts below the £5,000 a year point, in which case they were facing a progressive decline in real income, or if inflation carried them up to the magic £5,000 figure at which registration was obligatory, then 10 per cent (later reduced to 8 per cent) of their total income was mulcted by the State. This was felt as a particular injustice by those who were not free to set their fees at any level they wished. One example of the kind of absurd anomalies involved is that non-medical psychotherapists have to pay Value Added Tax. Medically qualified ones do not.

Clearly the first essential here is the raising of the V.A.T. exemption threshold (now £7,500), and its indexing subsequently. It is hard to see the Customs and Excise softening in their attitudes (though much more courtesy would not come amiss) particularly since one defect of the tax is the strict policing it requires. But if it is proper to pay Post Offices for their revenue-collecting activities on behalf of the State, is there not a case for some fee to be paid to the unwilling collectors of Value Added Tax?

This is perhaps the point to mention one exaction from the self-employed which, though perhaps not large in absolute terms, has done more to convince them that they are being unfairly treated than any other single measure. This is the new National Insurance arrangements which came into effect from April 1975. These involved the payment by the self-employed, in addition to their existing flat-rate National Insurance 'stamp', a new earnings-related contribution known as a Class Four contribution. This Class Four contribution is assessed and collected by the Inland Revenue. It amounts to 8 per cent of 'profits or gains' between £1,600 and £4,900. In brief, it means that any self-employed person making £3,600 pays an extra £160. If they make £4,900 or more they pay £264 extra.

There is always at one time one tax or impost that is felt as a special outrage. If savers bitterly resent, as they do, the investment-income surcharge, there is no doubt that the self-employed hate the Class Four contribution. The reason they do so is simple, as the official pamphlet explains. 'Class Four contributions will not entitle you to any extra benefit; their purpose is to ensure that the self-employed as a whole pay a fair share of the cost of pensions and other national insurance benefits.' Not surprisingly, this bland assertion has produced something like a state of shock among a good many self-employed people.

So far, this chapter has been virtually a catalogue of tax injustices bearing down upon the self-employed. In normal circumstances one might have hoped to take a wider view, but today the circumstances are not normal. It is the fiscal framework which overwhelmingly determines the prospects for small, private or one-man businesses. After all, there are two phases to the building of such a business or career. There is the exercise of ability or effort, and there is, one hopes, the accumulation of resources. The effect of the present tax structure is to make the first of these unrewarding, and the second more and more nearly impossible. One of my correspondents makes the point that, if one compares the jobs where there is no trade union organization, and no overtime – which on the whole involve the greatest skill, the longest training and the highest risk – then calculated at an hourly rate the work is often a good deal worse paid than that of relatively unskilled work – as any junior hospital doctor will testify.

Unfortunately, our catalogue of destructive tax changes is by no means finished yet. It is impossible to end this section without describing the destructive impact that Capital Transfer Tax, unless repealed, will have on the future of privately owned businesses in this country. This tax was passed into law in March 1975, though it applies to all gifts made from 26 March 1974. It replaces, with devastating effect, the old Estate Duty. The latter was a tax on capital which was payable only at one stage, death. The citizen could do what he liked with his capital during his life, though to be free of all tax, gifts had to be made more than seven years before death.

The effect of Estate Duty throughout its existence was to penalize those who clung on to their wealth to death and thus to encourage giving it away during life. The rates were in theory confiscatory but in practice bearable because of the exemption on gifts made more than seven years before death. The effects of Capital Transfer Tax are very different. All gifts made during the lifetime of the individual are added up (aggregated in the jargon of the taxman) and taxed upon a progressive scale. There is a lower limit of £15,000 which inflation is rapidly eroding and an apparent concession in the form of exemption on gifts between spouses, so that no wife has to pay duty on her husband's death. This, however, while welcome in itself, merely means that the Revenue take a larger bite on the death of the surviving spouse. If, however, this tax remains in force for any length of time, it will have a devastating effect on privately owned businesses, of which there are more than 800,000 in this country. Many of these, of course, are tiny in size – the corner newsagent, for example. If, however, the business is of any size, it is going to become virtually impossible to pass it on intact. There are two reasons for this. The first is that the tax is levied on a scale of severity unmatched anywhere else in the world. The second is more subtle. If £250,000 cash is transferred, say, to a son more than three years before death, then tax of £76,375 has to be paid, which, though heavy, can come out of the capital sum.

But suppose that a business worth £250,000 is to be transferred. The natural wish of the donor is for the business to remain intact. There is certainly unlikely to be loose cash floating around, but a procedure known as 'grossing-up' takes effect. That is to say, the donor is deemed to have transferred such sum as will after tax leave £250,000. Since the rates escalate incredibly quickly, the effect is mortal. For example, on a business valued for tax purposes at £200,000, more than £105,000 has to be paid. If the business were to be valued at £450,000, then tax of nearly £600,000 would have to be paid for it to remain intact. These, remember, are transfers more than three years before death. If the transfer is not made till death, the rates are still more lethal. Moreover, if previous gifts have been made to other people, perhaps before the business is transferred, all the gifts are added up so that the tax may start at an even higher rate (see Table 8).

Not surprisingly, the introduction of this tax brought a storm of protest from businessmen. The validity of this protest is surely shown by the fact that in April 1976, only one year after the tax was enacted, the Chancellor introduced a relief for businesses, family companies and working farmers, rather narrowly defined. A 30 per cent reduction is granted on the valuation of relevant

TABLE 8   Capital Transfer Tax

Net value of transfer	Tax				Tax expressed as percentage of net value of transfer	
£	£				£	
15,000	Nil	plus	5·26%	on next	4,750	Nil
19,750	250	,,	8·10%	,, ,,	4,625	1·26
24,375	625	,,	11·11%	,, ,,	4,500	2·56
28,875	1,125	,,	14·28%	,, ,,	8,750	3·89
37,625	2,375	,,	17·65%	,, ,,	8,500	6·31
46,125	3,875	,,	21·21%	,, ,,	8,250	8·40
54,375	5,625	,,	25·00%	,, ,,	16,000	10·34
70,375	9,625	,,	29·03%	,, ,,	15,500	13·67
85,875	14,125	,,	37·93%	,, ,,	14,500	16·44
100,375	19,625	,,	58·84%	,, ,,	19,500	19·55
119,875	30,125	,,	73·09%	,, ,,	28,750	25·13
148,625	51,375	,,	100·00%	,, ,,	25,000	34·57
173,625	76,375	,,	122·22%	,, ,,	22,500	43·99
196,125	103,875	,,	150·00%	,, ,,	80,000	52·97
276,125	223,875	,,	185·71%	,, ,,	175,000	81·07
451,125	588,875	,,	233·33%	,, ,,	300,000	121·66
751,125	1,248,875	,,	300·00%	on excess		

Note: Transfers of value made more than three years before death, transferor assuming liability to pay the tax.

business assets, or shares representing a controlling interest in a company. Working farmers, narrowly defined, can get relief of 50 per cent on agricultural property up to £250,000 in value or 1,000 acres in size. Above this point they should get the 30 per cent relief.

There is another possible way of reducing these appalling rates in the case of a business. If the person receiving the gift – the donee – makes it clear at the time of receiving it that he is accepting liability for the tax, then 'grossing-up' does not apply. Table 9 shows the more modest rates that apply in such a case.

Even so, the tax is, by any standards, swingeing. Moreover, although there are provisions in the case of land or shares in a

TABLE 9   Capital Transfer Tax

Gross value of transfer	Tax	Tax expressed as percentage of gross value of transfer
£	£	
15,000	Nil	0
20,000	250	1·25
25,000	625	2·5
30,000	1,125	3·75
40,000	2,375	5·94
50,000	3,875	7·75
60,000	5,625	9·38
80,000	9,625	12·03
100,000	14,125	14·13
120,000	19,625	16·35
150,000	32,125	20·08
200,000	51,375	25·69
250,000	76,375	30·55
300,000	103,875	34·62
500,000	223,875	44·77
1,000,000	548,875	54·89
2,000,000	1,248,875	62·44

Note: Transfers more than three years before death, tax paid out of property transferred or by donee. The rates applicable to lifetime transfers are lower than the rates charged upon death up to a total chargeable value of £300,000.

family business whereby the tax can be paid in instalments over eight years, interest is charged on the balance at the rate of 9 per cent, and the interest payments are not deductible for income tax purposes. It is hard to see very much comfort here. If this tax stays on the statute book for any length of time, it will be very hard to pass on a farm or family business intact. Indeed in December 1976 a statement by six leading business organizations, including the National Farmers' Union and the Unquoted Companies Group, declared that unless capital taxation were changed privately owned companies would be destroyed within a generation. It pointed out that against the maximum rate in the

U.K. of 75 per cent the highest rate on a transfer to children in direct line in E.E.C. countries was about 20 per cent.

These days there are two views of inheritance. One school of thought believes that each new generation should begin from scratch. I personally find the concept of this one-generation society profoundly unattractive, but this is not the point. What is surely undeniable is that the desire to build up an ongoing business is a very powerful motive and a very powerful incentive. Very few businesses of any size will be able to remain intact under this particular legislation. The results will be a further accretion of power to the State, a considerable change in the organization of private industry, and a profound disincentive to all who have hopes of creating something lasting in this field. There are other noteworthy provisions, such as the fact that Capital Gains Tax may be chargeable in addition to the Capital Transfer Tax. And finally there is the prospect of a Wealth Tax which may come on top of all this witches' brew. The Confederation of British Industry calculates that, on the lower of the two scales given in the Wealth Tax Green Paper, at the end of thirty-five years a business worth £500,000 initially would be worth only 44 per cent of its untaxed value. The prospect of Wealth Tax on land is, in some ways, still more daunting. Farmers are rarely people with free or excess capital. A Wealth Tax would take capital out of the farm year by year when official policy is to put capital in and build up home food supplies. What one can say is that Corporation Tax, high rates of personal income tax, Capital Transfer Tax and prospectively a Wealth Tax, taken individually, are profoundly discouraging to the self-employed. Taken together they amount to confiscation on an unprecedented scale.

This account is necessarily incomplete. There is the question of the rating system and its impact on small businesses. There is felt to be, and there is, an increasing bureaucratic interference. But for the tax system these things might be endurable. As it is, the self-employed feel harassed and discriminated against. They are profoundly disillusioned. They have every right to be so.

7 The battle of ideas

It is not difficult to chart the damage that has been done to the middle class by the combination of inflation and the tax system. But it has suffered equal casualties – and over a longer period – in the battle of ideas. Indeed, one is tempted to describe the losses suffered in this way as almost entirely self-inflicted. There are two reasons for this. The first is that the great scourges of the bourgeoisie from Marx to the modern sociologists are nearly all middle-class figures themselves; no one could be less proletarian than the advocates of proletarian revolution. There is nothing particularly surprising in this. One of the great functions of the middle class has, after all, been to provide much of the intellectual drive that has powered our civilization. It may have done this rather too successfully.

The second factor is the middle-class sense of guilt. It is a nice point whether this has been externally engendered by a century of attack and criticism or whether middle-class guilt feelings have a largely inward psychological cause. Any form of good fortune is liable to give rise to anxiety and fears of retribution; classically the Chinese would call a pretty child 'ill-favoured' for fear it would attract the jealousy and retribution of the gods. This possibly explains why the intellectual attack on the middle class has been so much more vigorous than its defence of itself. Those middle-class figures who purged their guilt by a complete repudiation of their own origins acquired a certain freedom thereby. As always though, when ideas filter down and filter through, an inevitable element of the banal is present. The end result of a century of propaganda, of the great intellectual battles of the past, is three banal notions that have coloured the thinking of a large part, though not all, of the middle class. The first is a simple defensiveness, a feeling that perhaps it is, after all, quite simply wrong for anyone to have anything which not everybody has. This imparts a kind of furtiveness to some middle-class life. One meets savers who feel guilty about saving, subscribers to private medical schemes who worry that they have chosen to devote part of their expenditure to this rather than any other purpose. This conditioned attitude is taken as natural by many. In a discussion on equality, for example, Professor John Vaizey says this:

> But if you ask why is it the case that people think that, given seven children and a cake, and if you know no more about the children than that they are children and they all like cake, then it seems 'natural' to give each one seventh of the cake and not to produce an unequal distribution? The answer is simply that it is so.[19]

I find this quotation fascinating because Professor Vaizey, a man of most distinguished intellect and reasoning powers, has, in his summing up of an extended discussion, simply failed to see that his answer is not self-evident.

If one discusses the division of the cake with children and not just with philosophers and social scientists, it is possible to arrive at quite a different answer. If the cake is small, in fact, ordinary, sensible children prefer not to divide it equally, because they know very well that they would each of them only get a crumb. In these circumstances children will choose one of their number to have it, maybe by an 'eeny-meeny-mo' method. They hope their turn will come. In other words anything that is regarded as self-evidently just or unjust in the area of distribution has a high chance of merely being the irrational prejudice of the moment. And the Vaizey quotation shows just what the irrational prejudice of today is.

The second banal notion is the idea of 'middle-classness' as something of which one should be ashamed. In the same series of discussions to which I referred, John Mackintosh, a Professor of Politics and Labour Member of Parliament, described an incident in which he had taken part:

> I remember coming out of a football match recently and being propelled by the crowd down a slope towards a bunch of policemen. There was nothing I could do about it and the police were worried about what might have been a dangerous situation. The first policeman grabbed me

and started to pull me towards a van. And I said, 'Look here, officer, this is not my fault,' and he immediately let go of me and grabbed the chap behind me who had a different accent. Now this was a simple little example of coercion in Britain, in a class-structured society. I didn't intend to play the class game, but I did. Immediately I spoke, the fellow thought, 'Right, this is a middle-class chap, the crowd behind is pushing him,' so he grabbed the bloke behind me who was a working man. The policeman was treating people unequally.

There are a number of comments which can be made about this. It is the job of policemen, after all, to treat people unequally, in the sense of arresting wrongdoers and letting ordinary members of the public go. The appreciation the policeman made of the situation, 'This is a middle-class chap, the crowd behind is pushing him,' is, on Mr Mackintosh's own showing, quite right. It was a very accurate assessment. Moreover – and this is the part that Mr Mackintosh finds so intolerable – it is a practical, empirical fact that middle-class people on the whole do not riot at football matches. In wishing to deny this important fact, he imputes a whole area of class bias to the police.

The third of these notions that colours so much thinking is, in fact, an extension of the second. It is the idea that anything that is middle class is automatically certainly of less than general validity and quite possibly very bad indeed. The key phrase in this context is 'middle-class values'. A rational person would seek to examine what the values of the middle class are and might find some of them admirable, and others less so. But the phrase 'middle-class values' is used in a doubly destructive fashion.

On the one hand, it is used to denigrate values which, at most times in history, have been felt to have great worth – respect for truth, the desire for objectivity, love of scholarship – as well as humbler ones such as a desire to see fair play and a belief in law and order. Then, as an extension of this, much of the traditional education of this country is attacked, on the grounds that it inculcates only middle-class values. The extreme or limiting case of this is, of course, provided by those Revolutionary Socialist teachers who regard it as their task to indoctrinate their children with 'militant working-class attitudes', for example, hatred of the police, love of the Shrewsbury pickets. But in a watered-down attitude, it is liable to lead to a feeling that schools should not require intellectually difficult studies since these are, or are believed to be, harder for working-class than for middle-class children. The end result of this, of course, as of so much of the attack on the middle class, is the infliction of a new form of deprivation on working-class people and their children.

As for the middle class's feelings of guilt, it is probably too much to hope that it can be freed completely from them. It is not too much, however, to point out its largely irrational nature. There seems to be a kind of rule that provides that the larger the quantum of middle-class guilt the less the justification for it. During the nineteenth century, when poverty was extreme and conditions of labour often intolerable, it was, until the rise of the Fabians, little in evidence. Only in the last twenty years of the century does the groundswell seem to have begun. More evident after the First World War, still more after the Second, rising to a high level during the enormous increase in national and particularly working-class prosperity in the fifties, the sense of guilt seems to have reached its peak in the present period of relative and absolute middle-class decline. Some middle-class thinkers indeed have noticed this important point, and have, therefore, transferred their guilt feelings from the condition of the working population in this country to that of the genuinely poor in the 'Third World'. Whether this poverty is their fault is another matter; they have to feel guilty about something.

Perhaps the most important single point about guilt is that it is by no means as highly unselfish an emotion as it seems. The person actuated by feelings of guilt is concerned essentially with his own psychic needs, not with the objective condition of those he feels guilty about. He helps them – if he does – not because they need help or ought to be helped, but to make himself feel better. A rational assessment of the situation can be incomparably more fruitful than the most luxurious feelings of guilt. In the case of the British middle class, such an assessment would show those feelings of guilt to be wholly unnecessary.

Middle-class *angst*, middle-class guilt feelings, are the subjective side of the battle of ideas. The objective attack has come mainly from two directions, the Marxists and the egalitarians, the hard liners and the soft.

Two quotations will, I think, serve to give the Marxist view of things. The first is from the Communist Manifesto: 'The executive of the modern state is but a committee for managing the common affairs of the whole bourgeoisie.' The second is from Lenin in *State and Revolution*: 'The forms of the bourgeois state are extremely varied but in essence they are all the same; in one way or another, in the last analysis all these states are inevitably the dictatorship of the bourgeoisie.' As Ralph Miliband, one of the most eloquent and perceptive Marxist apologists writing today, puts it:

> In one form or other the concept this embodies reappears again and again in the work of both Marx and Engels; and despite the refinements and qualifications they occasionally introduced . . . they never departed from their view that in capitalist society the state was above all the coercive instrument of a ruling class, itself defined in terms of its ownership and control of the means of production.[20]

Central to the Marxist world picture is the view of a ruling and exploiting class, first feudal, then bourgeois, with its hands on a totally disproportionate amount of wealth, owning and controlling the means of production and, in whatever disguise, using the coercive power of the State to maintain its position. From this it follows that there is an exploited class – the working class – and an inevitably continuing class struggle until, Marxists believe, the time when the working class achieves its inevitable victory, a class society ceases, and the State – eventually – withers away. Such a view does not, of course, exclude the existence of upward – and downward – mobility between the classes or of worsening conditions for the self-employed. Miliband himself seems to distinguish a large and growing class of professional people and those associated with small and medium-size enterprises which he makes a 'middle class', between the class which owns and controls, and the working class. But in general it is not a misrepresentation of Marxist theory to say that, if one is not being exploited, one is an exploiter.

This fits in perfectly with the middle-class sense of guilt. It must be pointed out, however, that in Marxist theory, 'exploita-tion' has a precise and technical meaning. Underpinning it is the Theory of Surplus Value, under which the only value that is added to goods comes from the work or labour that is put into their production. It follows, therefore, that profit, all profit, can only be obtained by withholding from the workers some part of the value they have created, and capitalism of any sort becomes, in the last analysis, a sort of legalized theft. Marxism as a theory is not without a certain scope and grandeur; it explains, or seems to explain, so much. And the view of profit as theft consciously or unconsciously underlies many of the characteristic attitudes of organized labour. It is worth pointing out, therefore, that there is no reason whatever to consider the Theory of Surplus Value to be true or indeed to take it seriously. It would require us to believe that, in a modern chemical plant or oil refinery, say, virtually entirely automated, in which the staff is reduced to a few score supervisors and maintenance men, their efforts and their efforts alone are the sole source of the profit that plant produces. It allots no reward to entrepreneurial skills, none to the provision of re-sources. And yet it remains a powerful myth.

One other aspect of the Marxist view deserves a comment here. The pioneers of communism, observing as they did the course of events in nineteenth-century Europe, predicted steadily increas-ing misery for the working class, and the unemployment of the inter-war years seemed to give some colour to this view. And yet with whatever pauses, whatever inadequacies, the past century has seen a tremendous rise in the average standard of living in the advanced industrial countries. We hear much criticism of the so-called 'consumer society' in which the public is said to be manipulated by advertising into 'wanting' unnecessary goods. No doubt it has its unattractive side, but if such a society exists at all, there is a vitally important conclusion to be drawn. The prosperity of the capitalists and the continued existence of a vast productive machine depends on mass markets, and mass markets depend on mass prosperity. On this view, businessmen, capitalists, the exploiting class in Marxist terminology, have a vested interest in increasing working-class prosperity. It is not necessary to impute any virtue to them for having this vested interest, but it does seem to me to cut a swathe through some cherished fields of Marxist theory. Let me add – though it is a separate topic – that, in this country at least, over the past decade, there is a strong case for saying that the share of the national income going to the factor of labour has been too high. Profit has been not too high but too low, and this has reduced not only investment but the real standard of living below that which could have been achieved.

The impact of the Marxist view should not be under-estimated. When the Labour Party seeks in its Constitution to nationalize the means of production, distribution and exchange, it is putting forward an aim that is justified only upon a Marxist view. And far more people are swayed by beliefs and prejudices that can be made sense of only upon a Marxist view than have ever sat down and studied Marx.

But the claims of the egalitarians are still more influential and, in my view, more immediately dangerous to the interests of the middle class. They are shared by many middle-class people, and it is hard not to feel that they are in accordance with the spirit of the age. People are much more aware of, much more uneasy about, differences than ever before. In times when society generally was incomparably poorer than today the Roman Catholic Church thought the display of wealth and pomp completely suitable for the service of God. Today the cardinals' trains are truncated and they are exhorted to simplicity by the Pope. Neither position is more logical than the other.

The non-Marxist intellectual case for egalitarianism rests upon two pillars. The first is a question of fact, the alleged fact being the existence of great inequalities in our society. The other is opinion, the opinion being that the inequalities observed ought to be reduced or eliminated. In *Socialism Now*, published as recently as 1974, Mr Anthony Crosland starts by saying:

> I observe that there exist extreme inequalities in Britain, which often stem not from hard work but from inheritance and the accident of birth, which are wholly irrelevant to the achievement of economic growth, which are punitive and discriminatory in their effect on the poorer classes and offensive to any canon of social justice.[21]

He then goes on to say that a practising politician is not required ultimately to decide how much inequality is acceptable; he has plenty of harsh, specific and unmerited inequalities to combat in the next ten years.

This passage seems to me to be a splendid example of fact and opinion inextricably mixed. I do not believe his facts are right, and I am sure his opinions are wrong. In earlier chapters I have attempted to show just how far the levelling-down process has gone; that is a question of fact. I believe that the most character-istic feature of the English sickness is an obsession with the distribution of wealth, never with its creation; that is a matter of opinion. But on the general question of equality the main point I wish to make is that there is no obvious moral superiority in either point of view, in wishing to see more equality or wishing to see less. Either point of view can be held sincerely for high-minded reasons; either point of view can be held for ignoble reasons.

But if there is no self-evident moral superiority in one view-point over the other, we are entitled to look at the claims of equality with a notably cold and fishy eye. We can observe that, nobly though the quest started, it seems rapidly to lead to some-thing not at all elevated. The early socialists seemed, in their hopes of equality, to mean a society in which everyone was mid-dle class in their standards, their ideals and their way of life. Now even equality of opportunity, a gentler ideal than equality *tout court*, and one with a wider appeal, is often pursued in a way which suggests that the doing down of the middle class is a stronger motive than the elevation of anyone else. This is particularly true in the field of educational controversy; schools, excellent in themselves, are condemned because of the advantages they are held to bring the middle class.

We are entitled to say that a society without choice, without diversity, would be a tyrannous society. It is also doubtful whether it would be a more contented one. As Samuel Brittan has pointed out:

It is no use saying that resentment and envy of the possessions and achievements of others, and strong views about people's life-styles simply exist, whether the liberal individualist likes it or not. The atti-tudes in question are influenced by what is said and written; and the contribution of the so-called intelligentsia is to focus all attention on relativities to the exclusion of absolutes. Moreover their object in so doing is not to stir up personal rivalry and emulation, which add to the interests and joys, as well as unhappiness of life; it is to emphasize differences while asserting that they should not be there.

He goes on (and I do not think the anti-egalitarian case has ever been better put):

If comparisons are always with other people and never with past achievements, the hope of progress is at an end . . . If we look at definite things, such as treatment of children, the level of nutrition, health, housing or consumption of the poorest . . . improvement is possible. In the realm of intangibles such as self-respect, improvement is more difficult but can still be envisaged; and this also applies to the reduction of coercion in human affairs. But if all that matters is whether other people are better or worse off than oneself in these respects, then human history is a zero sum game . . . [22]

The resentment and envy upon which the egalitarians, deliberately or not, have played are unlikely to diminish as the process of levelling down continues. On the contrary, one would expect envy to be enshrined as a way of life, and attention focused more and more minutely upon differentials. It is not too much of a nightmare to foresee the day when genetic differences, brightness against stupidity, or the benefits that a loving and cultured home background can confer on a child, are the source of just as much resentment as differences of income. Writing about equality, the sociologist A. H. Halsey used a phrase that I find curiously revealing. 'Rather over-dramatically, perhaps, one is seeking from fraternity', he wrote, 'something like a peaceful equivalent of war.'[23] I believe we should recognize that the egalitarian intelligentsia *is* making war, upon the stability of society and upon the middle class.

Marxism and egalitarianism are the two main ideological justifications of the war upon the middle class. But one further intellectual construct should not be overlooked. This is the idea, associated with a number of romantically minded sociologists, of a distinctive working-class culture embodying the strength and virtues of the nation. This is a view they are entitled to take, even if one believes that their glasses are rose-tinted. It does not concern us here, except insofar as it is used as a stick to beat the middle class with. The defence of the middle class does not require the denigration of any other group. It is odd that so-called friends of the working class should exalt it to decry their own background.

PART TWO
The fight back

8 Does the middle class matter?

Till this point I have been concerned with charting the erosion of the middle-class position, in terms of living standards, of ideas and of self-esteem. This is, I have no doubt, an essential task, but it is not without its dangers, especially the danger that the middle class can be depicted as a selfish, whining crew, concerned only to protect their own privileges.

This is, of course, a wonderful version of Catch 22: if the middle class says nothing it is acquiescing in its own destruction; if it protests it is demonstrating that it is not worthy to survive. In fact, the striking and remarkable feature about the post-war history of the past few years has been the patience and quietness of the middle class, the absence of protest during a long period of decline.

There are a number of reasons for this. The first, and most important, is quite simply a question of unselfishness. All too often the middle class is portrayed as a collection of monsters and selfishness, bitterly resenting social change and working-class prosperity. It would be foolish to deny that there have been resentments; among the correspondence I received, from which I selected the quotations in Chapter 2, there were a proportion of bitter and Blimpish letters. The surprising thing is, however, the smallness of that proportion. There has been a general recognition that social change had to come, and a readiness to acquiesce in its consequences. The fact that one third of the middle class habitually votes for the Labour Party suggests indeed that much of the middle class has been prepared even to hurry that change along. In some ways this is the positive aspect of the negative feelings of guilt discussed earlier, the idea of fairness counting for a great deal. There was in particular a failure to distinguish between the great increase in working-class prosperity, which any sensible person would welcome, and the increasing difficulties for the middle class. There was a tendency to assume that the one necessarily entailed the other, and that therefore because the first was desirable it would be wrong to cavil at the second.

Second, there was, and is, a great reluctance to discuss the matter in class terms. I don't say that class, like death, has become one of the great taboo subjects. I do say that many middle-class people feel that, if they identify themselves, if they discuss it in these terms, they are doing something disreputable, somehow sharpening conflict. It is as if they felt that they cannot praise themselves without dispraising the working class. When I published my original appeal for information in the paper, I received several letters, patently from middle-class people, begging me not to discuss the subject in terms of working class and middle class. I was using bad words and would, it seemed, make things worse and bring misfortune on us all if I insisted on discussing the matter in these terms. Such an attitude, it hardly needs saying, acts greatly to the detriment of the middle class. Those who disapprove of middle-class 'privileges', middle-class values and middle-class ways of living have no hesitation in briskly dividing society into working class and middle class. To reply feebly, 'Oh dear, I don't like thinking of matters in these terms,' is not going to stop other people doing so. It is an attitude of pusillanimity that merely encourages the critics of the middle class to press home the attack.

The danger here is that we are beginning to enter a world in which there is a simple equation, drawn from the realm of Orwellian Newspeak, in which Middle Class equals Bad and Working Class equals Good. Values have only to be described as Middle Class to be implicitly rejected. Let me give two examples of this in practice, culled from the *Guardian* newspaper on successive days.

The first comes from a report of a week's course for head and other senior teachers in London schools.

As far as the potential head's own attitudes to the outside world were concerned, the course left a feeling of some unease. The big influx of middle-class children into London's comprehensive schools is seen by some of their teachers as a threat. There was little feeling that, in some circumstances, skilled and articulate parents might actually be of use to a school – in raising funds at least, at best even providing some help in the specialist areas where teachers are in short supply.

Discussing the course afterwards with some of the participants, they were ready enough to discuss the profession's hang-ups. Several teachers admitted that life was simply easier for them when all the parents were working class. And this preference was mixed up with the very worthy feeling that their real concern should be with the most deprived children. This made it difficult for them to admit that the bright or the middle class could have problems too, or that they should have an equal claim to a teacher's time or attention.

Some even went so far as to admit to definite prejudice against the middle-class child, and this included their own children.[24]

We are really getting into a remarkable state in which middle-class parents feel and admit to a prejudice against their own children – because they are middle class!

The following day the *Guardian* carried a report of a religious occasion under the simple heading 'Middle-class church attacked'. It started:

The new General Synod of the Church of England, which was inaugurated yesterday with ecclesiastical pomp and the touch of worldly circumstance, was given a firm warning about its middle-class image.

Bishop John Howe, the secretary-general of the Anglican Consultative Council, which links the worldwide communion, told members of the Church's Parliament that middle-class Anglicanism had been exported ... it was an image that led to some states and post-colonial governments excluding Christianity from having an important role in their countries.[25]

What is one to say? Here we have not even middle-class values but 'a middle-class image' leading, according to the good Bishop, whole nations to reject the Christian religion. What a terrible thing a middle-class image must be!

And is it over-sensitive to notice a series of six B.B.C. television programmes entitled *Milestones in Working-Class History* (with book of same title)? Doubtless a worthy series but is one ever likely to see a sister series *Milestones in Middle-Class History*?

These factors, important as they are, are by no means the only reason for the absence of protest. To them one has to add a genuine and characteristic dislike of making a fuss. It is said that the quintessential middle-class remark is: 'I'm terribly sorry, but you're treading on my foot.' Then there is the sheer diversity of the middle class itself. It have argued that it is a very broad segment of the nation, but it is hard to imagine the owner of a corner shop and the Harley Street surgeon feeling they had much in common – beyond, in both cases, an extremely busy existence which leaves them little time for meetings, protests and the like.

Each of these factors is important. John Gorst, M.P., founder of the Middle Class Association (of which more later), was driven by his experiences to enunciate Gorst's Law. This is based on his conviction that the middle class is made up of independent people who do not easily join together. According to the law, only 'if the external threat is greater than the sum total of their internal differences do you get unity'.

At this point, however, a central issue, almost the central issue of this book, has to be faced. One can chart the decline of the middle class in economic terms. One can demonstrate that it is desperately anxious, much given to guilt, increasingly sneered at and attacked. Sooner or later the question has to be asked:'Are the critics right? Does it deserve all that it gets?'

We have come a long way from the days when it was taken for granted that the strength of the nation lay in a numerous, independent and prosperous middle class. Nowadays I think any attempt to vindicate the middle class has to follow two main paths. The first is to show that its independent existence does not harm the nation or individuals. The second is to demonstrate the positive benefits it brings to individuals and the nation.

In order to pursue the first line of enquiry and show that the middle class is not positively harmful one has to start, I think, by clearing away a little of the intellectual rubbish of the age. One has to begin by examining some of the verbal usages of today and the assumptions that lie behind them. As good a point as any to start with is the word 'privilege' used, as it so often is, as a pejorative description of differences. Behind this, of course, is the idea that it is totally wrong for anyone to have anything if everybody else cannot have it as well. Partly this is pure, simple envy, partly something, to my mind, even less attractive. The intolerance of diversity is rapidly reaching a point where there is a constant attempt to narrow the number of ways it is permissible to spend one's income. Private spending on health or on education is under severe and constant attack, as if to want something different, or better, or simply more private or convenient, than the State is in a position to provide is somehow morally wrong. Even saving, the habit of thrift insofar as it is not destroyed by inflation, is, as we have seen, capable of being resented as giving the person who saves an unfair advantage over the person who does not. And certainly to save for one's children, to wish to build something that lasts longer than one's own life-time, to pass on an inheritance, this is under almost equal attack. The only form in which wealth or fortune appears not to be resented is when it owes nothing to the exertions of the beneficiary or his predecessors. The uncovenanted win on the football pools or from premium bonds arouses no general disapprobation. Indeed the pools winner, chosen by fate or fortune, becomes a popular hero as the beloved of the gods.

'Inequality' as such is a concept discussed in the last chapter. Here it is merely necessary to say that it is only one sort of inequality that is objected to. Inequality of height, of athletic skill, of expectation of life, these it appears are permissible at least until sexual reproduction is abandoned in favour of reproduction by clones or cell cuttings, which one understands would produce an infinite number of completely identical persons. This would be enormously attractive to some future dictator, since it would iron out all differences that make populations of ordinary human beings tiresomely difficult to control.

This, in fact, gives us a clue. Equality, in the sense that it is used by the sociologists, the socialists and the would-be social engineers, is nothing more nor less than a recipe for tyranny.

Next there is the question whether, by its mere existence, that one third or more of the nation that is middle class is depriving the 60 per cent or less that is not of something that is rightfully theirs. I hope the analysis of the figures provided in the early part of this book disposes of the notion that there is anything worth a row of beans to be gained by pushing redistribution from the point it has reached to its ultimate conclusion. It is likely that the contrary is true. If I am right in thinking that thrift – saving for relatively long-term goals – is the central middle-class character-istic, then through saving, the middle class is conferring a sub-stantial and, indeed, vital benefit upon society as a whole. No economist would deny the central importance of private savings to the economy and no politician that the alternative quite simply is to achieve the same result by taxation. Those who save more than the average are giving those who save less than the average *their* freedom to spend their money as they wish, free from further forced saving by the State. There remains the possibility that 'middle-class values' which are spoken of with such venom, are, in some ways, positively harmful to society. Here there is less that can usefully be said, if only because we are entirely in the realm of value judgments, and if people find certain sets of values wholly distasteful it is very difficult to argue with them. One would have thought that some 'middle-class values' – insistence on the importance of education, a desire that one's children should be truthful, clean and well-mannered – would be quite non-controversial – if one had not heard them attacked by some educationists. Certainly they are values that many sections of the community, regardless of class, share. Some of them indeed are values that the Soviet Union is trying very hard to inculcate into the less advanced sections of its population.

The other main group of 'middle-class values' centres round a belief in self-help, self-reliance and the virtues of individual effort. There are obviously circumstances in which placing weight on objectives such as these may lead to smugness, but few people now would hold the nineteenth-century belief that prosperity can be equated with virtue and thus poverty with sin. In any case, it is hard to think of circumstances in which the pursuit of these goals can be held to be contrary to the interests of society as a whole.

So far I have been concerned to repel attacks. At the very least the middle class is entitled to reassert and take its stand on a principle of the 'felicific calculus' that the new puritanism – the puritanism of envy – is in danger of making us forget. It is the principle that if an action harms no one and benefits someone, then it cannot possibly be wrong. But it is time to assert the positive virtues of middle-class existence, and of the existence of the middle class. The middle class contains a very large proportion of the wealth-creators, of the innovators and those who give employment to others. It includes the great majority of the self-employed, and of the owners of small businesses. It is accused of philistinism, and yet it is both the originator and the transmitter of the high culture of our civilization. Here I will call as witness Mr J. B. Priestley, who writes:

... this egalitarian drive increases the pressure, already very severe, on our middle class. The full effect on our culture, largely based on the middle class, has not been felt yet, but many of us are feeling gloomy about our prospects.

I write here as an unrepentant bourgeois, knowing very well that the art and thought of Western Europe have come mostly not from aristocrats, peasants and workers but from the so often despised bourgeoisie.[26]

I personally do not want a homogeneous, even a homogeneously middle class, society, I want a type of freedom in which those who like responsibility can take it, and those who abhor it need not. But between the ideals of those early socialist pioneers whose Utopia was a kind of universal middle-class existence, with everyone prosperous, well dressed and opera-loving, and the ideals of those latter-day socialists who dream of a universal proletarianism, I know which I prefer.

Finally I would assert that freedom, both political and individual, depends in large measure on the strength and prosperity of the middle class. This is historically true and there is no reason to assume that it is less true today than it has been in the past. It is not just that were it to disappear then all power would inevitably centre in the State; in place of its 'privileges' would emerge a new and far more odious privileged class, entry to which depended entirely on being a member of, or in good standing with, the ruling bureaucracy. The existence of such middle-class enclaves of 'privilege' as private schools and private medicine is of great importance to the freedom of many millions of people who may never use them. While they exist there is an alternative to the State monopoly, the power of which is thus curbed. When they are gone, there will still be better forms of education, special

hospital treatment and the like, but only for the latter-day com-
missars, their families and associates. Independence of mind, the
diffusion of economic power, the diffusion of political power;
these are inextricably bound up with the existence and prosperity
of the middle class.

It should not be necessary, but it probably is, to add that these
assertions do not remotely have the effect of denigrating the non-
middle class. We are seeking to do no more than redress the
balance. I do not think anyone is in danger of under-estimating
the importance or the power of organized labour. But to say that
the country could not run without it, or that a general strike
would be devastating, is to say nothing. In every healthy society
there is a high degree of interdependence. Even from the limited
example of industrial action by junior hospital doctors, it is clear
that a strike by the professional classes, let alone the middle class
as a whole, would be just as devastating. But to say this is to say
nothing except that we depend on each other. The closest analogy
is perhaps the feminist call for a strike by women or wives to
show how indispensable they are. Of course it would show this. So
would a strike by men or husbands.

A society without the contribution of the middle class would be
infinitely poorer and not only in a material sense. It is time the
constant denigration ceased.

9   Can organizations help?

Throughout the twentieth century there have been intermittent attempts to organize the middle class into some form of pressure group. As far back as 1906 there was formed the Middle Classes Defence Organisation which, according to *The Times*, 'helped to bring victory to moderate candidates in the 1907 L.C.C. elections'. After the First World War the Middle Class Union arose, which according to Lewis and Maude actually became the British Branch of (of all unlikely things) the Middle Class International, which got as far as holding a Conference in Switzerland. The Middle Class Union – renamed the National Citizens' Union – was still in existence as late as 1942.

It is clear that none of these bodies has prospered and none has had the slightest impact on the course of events. But whenever the pressure on the middle class is felt to undergo sharp increases then the dream revives itself. 'If only', it goes, 'the middle class were organized.'

We have already seen just how Mr Denis Healey chose to treat the middle class in his Budgets of 1974. Not surprisingly, therefore, 1974 saw not one but two entirely new organizations spring into existence determined to act as its saviours. Before we ask how the middle class can help itself, it is well worth looking at these two organizations for the light that their history and progress throws on the problems.

The first of these organizations was born in November 1974 as The Middle Class Association. It was the brainchild of Mr John Gorst, a Conservative Member of Parliament, who was later associated with Mrs Margaret Thatcher's successful challenge for the leadership of the Conservative Party, and who had considerable experience of pressure groups. Mr Gorst would count among his previous successes a campaign for local commercial radio stations, and the formation of the Telephone Users' Association – the latter perhaps a pyrrhic victory since it has not prevented the quality of the service declining.

The Middle Class Association, which officially dates from 11 November 1974, had as its aims:

1. To represent the interests of individuals who are self-employed or in professional, creative or managerial occupations (whether apprenticed, active or retired).
2. To take whatever action may be deemed necessary to further the interests of members.
3. To pursue these matters, either separately or in co-operation with other bodies, in whatever legal manner seems appropriate for their achievement.

A more detailed statement issued to founder members declared:

The basic malaise common to individuals who find themselves in the categories listed above can be summarized by saying that the economic policies followed by successive Governments since the Second World War have deprived them of a fair return for their industry, enterprise or thrift.

Inflation has removed the rewards from these individuals, while high government spending has fallen on them more heavily and more unfairly than is tolerable or equitable for any section of the working population – especially as they constitute a section without which the other, interdependent sections of the nation's work-force could not hope to prosper or even survive.

What is involved here is not the preservation of sectional supremacy, or even the differentials which have been eroded more by the bargaining power of organized labour than by any consideration of social justice. What is at stake is the survival of an essential element in the working population as a whole. Indeed failure to preserve this element and its interests will inevitably lead remorselessly to a collectivist society and the loss of individual liberty.

Mr Gorst was moved to act because he believed that there were two or three years at the most before the point of no return was reached. His message proved apparently well-timed. A great deal of publicity was attracted, a Steering Committee was rapidly set up, and the administration was undertaken by Mr Gorst in collaboration with a friend of his of long standing, Captain Willie Orr, a former Northern Ireland M.P.

At first all seemed to go well. By February 1975 the Association was able to issue a cheerful interim report; this included an analysis of the first thousand members, showing that they were drawn from every county in England, as well as Wales, Scotland and Northern Ireland, and came from a total of 214 different occupations.

Apart from general press publicity, the main aim of the Association at this time was to build up a large body of founder members, each of whom paid £5 as an initial subscription. The method by which they were recruited was principally by direct-mailing 'shots'. Mr Gorst had an expertise in this and this method proved cheaper than others tried, such as newspaper advertising; but its particular advantage in his view was that the costs could be carefully controlled. It could be shown how much each member cost to recruit.

Even while the Association was apparently going ahead there was an uneasiness in its ranks about the name. The fatal reluctance of the middle class to be thus identified was evident from the beginning in letters from members asking for a change of name, and there were even some people, though only a handful, who refused to join because they disliked the use of the word 'class'. Before long, a new name was announced – 'Voice of the Independent Centre'. Honourable though the organizers' motives were in thus renaming the Association, the new title seemed an anaemic one, and to some outside observers the fact that any change was made indicated something between diffidence of attitude and downright pussyfooting.

By the late summer membership was in excess of 4,000, but at this point two problems emerged. The first was that the direct-mail method of recruitment, though effective, was undoubtedly expensive. The membership increased but the funds did not, and Mr Gorst found himself under fire from members of the Steering Committee who were disappointed at the failure of the Association's bank balance to rise. Second, there began to be a pressure from activists within the Steering Committee for some kind of dramatic militant action.

The only dramatic and militant action came in the shape of a palace revolution within the Steering Committee. Mr Gorst, who had regarded its role as only advisory until such time as a full-scale organizing body could be elected by the entire membership, missed a meeting owing to the fact that he was moving house. At the meeting the Chairman, Mr Richard Holt, was removed from office and a new 'General Council' set up. Mr Holt was invited to be chairman of this, and Mr Gorst to be a member, but a new 'strong man' emerged. All executive decisions and the appointment of all officers were to be at the absolute discretion of Mr Joey Martyn-Martin, a flamboyant, naturalized Irish millionaire. To cap all this, a group of Steering Committee members registered Voice of the Independent Centre in their own names, thereby giving themselves control over the title.

Mr Gorst reacted immediately and angrily. In effect he washed his hands of the Association. Mr Martyn-Martin's major concern was with the threat of Communism, and Mr Gorst feared he would turn the Association quite simply into a militant extreme right-wing organization. In the event he did not turn it into anything. By November 1975 Mr Martyn-Martin had transferred his allegiance to a Brussels-based organization where, he said, 'I am not hampered by committees,' and which was satisfactorily 'hard-line anti-communist'. His resignation was reported on 5 November and, six days later, the *Daily Telegraph* announced under the heading 'One-year-old middle-class group dies' that Mr Richard Holt had resigned as chairman with the words, 'Our efforts have foundered to the point where I cannot see any future for the organization. I will certainly not be renewing my subscription.' Two days later the appointment of a new chairman was announced, but failing a miracle the Voice of the Independent Centre seemed to be limping towards oblivion.

The other organization that sprang into existence in 1974 was the National Federation of Self-Employed. It can be argued that the omens for this organization were a good deal more propitious; there are very nearly two million self-employed people in Britain, most of them feeling oppressed for the reasons set out earlier in this book. More important, most of them feel a stronger bond of mutual self-interest and mutual solidarity than does the middle class as a whole. Nonetheless, as we shall see, the history of the Federation has been to date a stormy one.

It was founded in Lytham St Anne's, Lancashire, on 15 September 1974. The founder, Mr Norman Small, a retired army captain and formerly an area recruiting officer for the small shopkeepers' unions, later said that he had the idea of founding the Federation while playing golf one day; it suddenly occurred to him that the self-employed had a lot to complain about – and no one to do the complaining for them. Accordingly, he advertised the idea in a local paper and, together with a few acquaintances and interested parties, held the first public meeting in his home town.

There can be no doubt that one specific grievance, more than anything else, provided the spark for the Federation and the key to its remarkable growth. This was the extra 8 per cent National Insurance contribution levied on the self-employed. This was the flash-point that brought members pouring in. This grievance provided the incentive to join, but Norman Small undoubtedly had the two qualities needed to start the organization off, one being what has been described as 'an undoubted flair for emotive public speaking' and the other, 'organizing ability'.

Within a few weeks, press and public were beginning to take an interest, and Mr Small's flat was engulfed in enquiries from potential members. Well before Christmas he, with one or two colleagues, notably Mr Gerry Parker-Brown, a local grocer, had begun to tour the country, whipping up enthusiasm and encouraging others to set up branches. By the end of the year, membership was approaching 10,000, necessitating the establishment of a Head Office – in fact a small office in the square at St Anne's-on-Sea. Finance was not, at this stage, a problem. Mr Small had wisely set the subscription high – it stood at the not inconsiderable figure by conventional standards of £12 a year. Policy *was* possibly more of a problem. 'Abolish the 8 per cent' was still virtually the only plank in the platform; the other main grievances expressed by members concerned V.A.T., a grinding headache for most small traders, and the whole question of rates, bureaucracy and form-filling.

The organizers recognized that they had to have a policy, but all such considerations tended to be submerged by the sheer physical difficulties of coping with recruitment and organization. Norman Small would go round the country speaking at public meetings. Most ended with the setting up of a new branch, and by the spring some 200 were in existence, membership was at the 15,000 mark and more than 200 new applications were coming in each day. A mass lobby of Parliament in March generated still further national publicity, and the period March–July 1975 was one of maximum growth. A network of twenty-eight regions plus Scotland and Northern Ireland was established. This made organization no easier – the National Executive consisted of the Chairman of each region plus *ex officio* members, so that it rarely numbered less than forty. This was clearly too large and too unwieldy for effective control and so it delegated its powers to a twelve-member Management Committee.

So far so good; Parliament was certainly becoming increasingly aware that the self-employed were unhappy, but at this stage difficulties began to emerge. The policy issue refused to be submerged. 'Abolish the 8 per cent' may have been a splendid slogan initially, but it hid a growing disagreement. Some of the more sophisticated members felt it was not a particularly strong plank, and one on which the Federation would find it difficult to get its way completely. They believed it better to press merely for tax relief on the contributions (at present they have to be paid out of taxed income). But many thousands of members had joined precisely because of this slogan and some regions were even on the verge of breaking away. Officially the policy is now to press for tax relief, but observers close to the Federation think the split could re-erupt at any time, even to the extent of disrupting the Federation. By this time, fortunately, there was a full-time Research Officer and it was possible to make reasoned presentations about such matters as V.A.T.

Even more alarming than the policy divisions, however, was the fact that a whole series of personality disputes began to rack the Federation and became public knowledge towards the end of the summer. A break-away Reform Group was founded by various disillusioned ex-officers of the Federation. Mr Small, the Founder-President, reported in the press as having had 'a complete collapse' after incessant travelling from meeting to meeting on a diet of pep-pills, resigned on grounds of ill-health, leaving a power vacuum at the top. The Honorary Secretary resigned after bitter disputes about the extent of his authority. A £6,000-a-year Chief Executive Officer was appointed, but he found himself the subject of much criticism and was eventually dismissed. Publicity, which had helped to create the Federation, threatened to destroy it as the various rows provided splendid copy for the press. Inevitably there were allegations of financial mismanagement – an alarming proportion of the £500,000 raised by the Federation since its formation seemed to have been spent; only £140,000 was said to be in the kitty in September 1975, plus £60,000 in a benevolent fund.

It would be wrong, however, to write the Federation off. The Party Conferences gave it a considerable boost. Jeremy Thorpe and Cyril Smith addressed a packed meeting organized by the Federation at the Liberal Party Assembly, while Margaret Thatcher spoke at a reception at the Conservative Party Conference. 3,000 self-employed people attended a rally in London and handed in to Downing Street a petition with 250,000 signatures. Moreover, the Federation was taken sufficiently seriously by the Customs and Excise and the Treasury to be accepted as a negotiating body.

By the autumn of 1975 membership, in spite of all difficulties, was close to 50,000. The key questions were whether the local organizers, of whom there were around 350, would be able to compensate by their steadiness for the ructions at the centre and whether they would get existing members to sign on for a second year. If – and only if – this could be achieved, then the Federation could settle down to a steady long-term future. At the time of writing, it is too soon to be certain of the outcome, but in 1976 there seemed to be a high rate of renewals, guaranteeing a continuing membership in excess of 45,000. The government undoubtedly helped by announcing a further increase in the maximum self-employed National Insurance contribution. It does have one very important factor working in its favour. The self-employed are undoubtedly under-represented, indeed virtually unrepresented, in the political system. Both the Conservatives and Liberals are becoming aware of their plight, and therefore any body which can genuinely claim to represent them has very great potential muscle.

The story of these two organizations well represents the problems and the opportunities facing any organizations for the middle class. John Gorst now believes that his organization aimed too wide. He does not think that there is room for a mass organization of the middle class. Were he to be starting the Middle Class Association again, he says, he would avoid a branch organization and aim to recruit perhaps 1,000 well-informed people to act as an intellectual pressure group.

He is almost certainly right in his self-criticisms. There is no single tie to bring together under one banner the enormous diversity of the middle class as such. Its members, although many of them are born organizers, do not organize themselves easily or well. They are reticent people and they are busy people. Moreover, any organization in its early stages – as the history of the National Federation of Self-Employed proves – though it may attract able and fiery founders, is also liable to attract the eccentric, the self-publicizing and the ambitious. Early committees are nearly all, in the nature of things, self-appointed – hence the frequent disruptions.

One of John Gorst's early ideas was to attempt to bring together under one umbrella as many organizations as possible concerned with the interests of people in professional, self-employed, farming and small business occupations. The aim was not to merge them, but merely to see if they could unite on a non-political basis to press for certain commonly agreed objectives. Invitations were sent out to no less than thirty such organizations. Representatives from twenty of them met in April 1975 at the House of Commons and a working party was set up to see what specific issues the individual organizations might have in common. The working party listed a number of topics ranging from inflation to the incidence of taxation. However, when it reported back to a further meeting of representatives which, interestingly, only ten organizations attended, the whole effort came to nothing. There was no agreement that enough organizations wanted to work together and, in the end, it was not even considered worth taking minutes of this final meeting.

On the other hand, specific organizations for specific purposes can work extraordinarily well. Perhaps the classic example of one of these was the Wing Airport Resistance Association (W.A.R.A.), formed to resist the idea of siting the proposed third London airport at Wing, in Buckinghamshire. (Wing, Stewkley and Cublington were three major villages in the area that would have been swallowed up.)

W.A.R.A. is often quoted as a quintessentially middle-class protest group, often, for that reason, with disapproving undertones. This is a complete misrepresentation. W.A.R.A.'s extraordinary success had two main reasons. One is that it did not merely oppose Cublington as a site, but suggested Foulness, off the Kent coast, as an alternative. The other was that it genuinely represented the passionate feelings of the overwhelming majority of the people in that area. That said, there is no doubt that it was able to draw on a very large and varied amount of middle-class skills. The chairman, Desmond Fennell, was a very able barrister; whatever skill was required it seemed to be on tap, whether it was Johnny Dankworth and Cleo Laine to provide music at rallies, or the Rector of Dunton (yet another local village) to bless and curse.

Two features of the campaign, which led to the overturning of the recommendation of the Roskill Commission to site the airport at Wing, seem particularly relevant to other possible protests. First, what one might call the 'public relations' aspect of the campaign was brilliantly successful. This was not due to the employment of expensive, or indeed any, professional public relations consultants, who were engaged only, and not notably successfully, to circularize M.P.s at one specific point in the campaign. What happened was that the amateurs concerned, being passionately committed, came up with idea after idea, such as a tractor drive (on a bitterly cold day) round the perimeter of the proposed airport, and – which was most moving of all – the placing of a lighted candle, symbolizing hope, on the last night of the Roskill hearings, in the windows of homes that would be affected.

Second, although W.A.R.A. engaged counsel to argue its case before the Roskill Commission, and though it mobilized public support through its activities, ultimately it was on the political front that its battle was won. It persuaded M.P.s and ultimately it persuaded Ministers. That is what counts in the end.

At this point a brief recapitulation may be of value. We have seen that the middle class comprises well over one third of the population of Britain, and there is evidence that, in spite of constant attacks by its critics, its aspirations are shared by a still larger section of the community. It believes both its values and its material standards to be under severe and increasing attack. Till recently a combination of altruism and a sense of guilt have caused it to accept its decline with a surprising degree of meekness, but during the past four or five years the pressure has increased to a point where it is felt by many to be intolerable. However, the middle class is not united; its diversity, a strength from many points of view, is, for purposes of protest, a weakness; its faith is traditionally in individual rather than collective action. Moreover, as the last chapter showed, attempts to organize a protest movement have, in the past, been conspicuously unsuccessful, unless there was some specific, well-defined goal to be achieved.

How then can it reasonably expect to protect itself from further attack, let alone to regain some of the ground that has been lost?

I think we have to start with a hard saying. A social class, like an empire, a nation, a religion or an economic system, lasts as long as, and no longer than, it has faith in itself. The smugness of the Victorian empire-builders, the self-confidence of the Victorian bourgeoisie, may seem strange and even laughable to us, but it is no coincidence that they were the characteristic attitudes of mind when both Empire and middle class were at their apogee. These frames of mind have gone for ever, and few would wish, even if it were possible, to recapture them. But there is always a loss. The psychic wrench caused by Britain's objective decline to somewhere well in the middle rank of powers militarily, and somewhere well below that economically, has given rise to a kind of strange self-hatred, the phenomenon which leads to yelps of delight at every new humiliation from Suez on. The decline of the middle class may have something to do with the strident middle-class criticism of the middle class, but on the whole, as I have argued, it has been received with great docility. The great question is whether the confidence of the middle class itself has been shattered beyond repair, or whether the vanished smugness and certitudes of former years can be replaced with a more rational belief in its own worth.

Only time can provide an answer to this question. Speaking personally, I feel a fair degree of optimism. The British are a profoundly bourgeois nation, and deep habits of thought are not eradicated overnight. In spite of all the sneers, more people believe they are middle class than objectively can be so regarded and still more people wish to be middle class than regard themselves as so being. Also, it is a characteristic, I believe, of the British to be very slow to anger. There seems to be a degree of inhibition in the national character that means that aggression is locked up until some extreme outrage or misfortune occurs. Not till Dunkirk do we feel free to fight back, but when our feelings are finally released they are correspondingly powerful. In the case of the middle class it is impossible to predict what the flashpoint will be. It can be something trivial, almost irrelevant, but the deep anger of the self-employed over the 8 per cent National Insurance levy well indicates how suddenly, without warning, and certainly without any possibility of prediction, an issue can arise.

But for middle-class protest to be effective it has to purge itself of three highly characteristic attitudes. The first is the characteristic middle-class feeling of guilt (discussed in Chapter 7). The psychologist Jung once suggested that the characteristic high Roman melancholy, to which so many ancient writers attest, had its roots in the fact that ancient Romans lived in a slave society and at an unconscious level identified with the slaves. We are not living in a slave society. If middle-class guilt arises from memories of long generations of overworked domestics, that is a sin that has been surely purged by now. If its roots are still deeper and less rational than that, the more reason why it should not be allowed to affect our actions.

Second, it is necessary to shuck off the uneasy feeling that by merely *being*, the middle class is, in some sense, doing the working class down. Economically speaking, the opposite is much nearer the truth. Redistribution has reached a stage where it is inhibiting the creation of wealth; this is not a difficult point to put over since most people will readily accept that wealth has to be created before it can be enjoyed. It is a concept, however, that has astonishingly little effect on how we think about our society or how we organize our affairs.

Third, it is vital to overcome the characteristic diffidence to which I referred earlier. Most of us can accept the view that a classless society would be a desirable ideal, and even if we do not accept the notion that Britain is a uniquely class-ridden society we can wish to see class distinctions further diminished and society become still more open and mobile. It is a long stride from this to the notion that for the middle class to assert its rights and its demands is in some way to strengthen class barriers. No one can say what forms future social organization will take. But I am quite sure that, for the middle class to be prepared to surrender its achievements, its values and its aspirations, would be an unforgivable betrayal, not only of itself, but of the whole nation. Insofar as middle-class attitudes are solid and enduring, the nation would be poorer without them. The idea of many early socialists, at least in this country, of a kind of universal adoption of middle-class attitudes, middle-class standards of living and middle-class values as their hoped-for millennium may seem curiously dated; one would hope for more diversity and a greater cross-fertilization in ideas and attitudes. It is a useful reminder, however, that, just as those who enjoy political freedom hold it in trust for those not yet or not at present able to experience it, so if the middle class vanish in a universal proletarianization it is the proletariat (however alien the word may sound on English lips) that would be the poorer for it.

What in short I am asserting is that in a political or social context self-abnegation is not a virtue. The first positive step, therefore, is for the middle class to recognize that, in the modern world, it is a pressure group like any other and it is legitimate for it to assert its own interests. One of the ways through the ramifications of modern politics is to see the system as government by pressure groups, with Governments not so much acting in accordance with long-devised strategies as responding to pressures, in part from immediate events, in part from groups of voters. The process is a healthy enough one. Groups of voters make their demands and the Government responds to them. It may not be particularly edifying, but the alternative, a system in which the Government is unresponsive to the pressures upon it, is far less attractive.

From this point of view, then, if there is a failure to exert pressure, this is not merely bad for the group concerned, whose interests will go by default. It is also bad for the body politic. It is a far worse society in which a Government has to listen only to what the T.U.C. wants, without any countervailing power, than one in which other interests in society assert the line beyond which they cannot be forced back.

The next important question is how is the middle class to exercise pressure? In the last chapter, I suggested that there was little future for mass organizations, with the exception of the National Federation of Self-Employed. The individualism, lack of time and sense of the ridiculous of the British middle class made it very unlikely even if it were desirable that some Poujadist political grouping would stand any chance. At the same time, it is quite clear that, in the last resort, it is in the political arena that battles are fought and won, as the story of Cublington shows. The most fatal thing that the middle class could do, next to refusing to fight at all, would be to turn its back on politics, because of feelings of disappointment or disgust where it feels that none of the existing political parties have catered adequately to its interests. Before the first of the two 1974 general elections I received many, many letters from members of the public expressing the sentiment 'A plague on both their houses'. If this resentment was translated into voting behaviour, then its sole result will have been to put Mr Wilson and his destructively egalitarian colleagues into office.

Pressure can only be exerted through the parties. It is no part of the purpose of this book to seek to impose a set of political beliefs upon the reader. It is, however, legitimate to point out that the prevailing philosophy of the Labour Party, unlike that of many Social Democratic parties in Europe, is deeply antipathetic to the interests of the middle class. From this point of view, I see the active egalitarians, with the late Mr Crosland as their philosopher-king, as more immediately dangerous and destructive than the woollier left-wing thinkers associated with Mr Wedgwood Benn and Mr Heffer. One may hope that one day the Labour Party may evolve into a reformist social democratic group on the continental model but there are precious few signs of it at present, and if I am right about the trend of events, then by the time this happens, if ever it does, it will be too late for the middle class.

The middle class has, therefore, two political tasks: to make the Labour Party aware of its irreducible demands, and the Conservative Party, which should be its natural ally, more responsive to its interests. (This is by no means the same thing as making it simply a middle-class party, which its leaders are sensibly concerned to avoid.) On the first count the militancy of the medical profession, faced with the plan to phase out pay beds from National Health Service hospitals, is one possible model. The key point here is that the consultants' action is not basically about pay but about an issue of principle. Many doctors in specialities such as psychiatry where there is virtually no opportunity for private practice none the less fully supported their colleagues because they saw the issue as involving the whole future organization of medicine in this country. In the winter of 1975 they embarked upon a policy of treating emergencies only. I would personally much prefer what may prove to be the next stage in this – and related disputes – that the doctors should resign wholly from the Health Service and, pending a settlement, treat patients on a basis of need, letting those who can pay and treating those who cannot free. Such a policy would combine the minimum inconvenience to the public with the maximum pressure on the Government. It does not, therefore, involve an abandonment of middle-class values or of the high ideals of the medical profession. After all, if the T.U.C. is able successfully to assert that Mr Heath's industrial relations policy – passed into law – is intolerable to it, then it is open to the doctors to demonstrate that Mrs Castle's medical policy, not then enacted, was equally intolerable to them.

As far as the Conservative Party is concerned, the accession of Mrs Thatcher to the party leadership is likely to have a double effect. It is a large – one would like to be able to say decisive – step away from Heath-type policies which involved so much sacrifice of middle-class interests in the hope of gaining trade union collaboration, and which seemed to be leading towards an unholy Government–T.U.C.–C.B.I. Corporate State-type alliance. It also marks a move towards attempting to limit the amount of Government, and the proportion of the national income that Government spends. Both these moves are in the interests of the middle class as well as of the nation as a whole. Much of Conservative policy is now in the melting pot, and it is up to the middle class to convince the new leadership that its instincts are sound, and that it will be actively supported in the constituencies and the country in boldly moving away from collectivism towards individualism.

When a Conservative Government is next returned to power, however, there is a vital need to ensure that middle-class needs do not get overlooked in the welter of problems and of conflicting interests that beset any Government. It is for this reason that I believe it important to campaign for the inclusion in the Government of a Minister for the Middle Classes. There is no substitute for a friend at court. The mere appointment of such a Minister would be an immense reassurance, for example, to the self-employed that their interests would be taken into account. His role could be both negative and positive. The negative role would consist of scrutinizing the policies of other departments for effects detrimental to the middle class, and then at least having an inter-departmental argument instead of it going by default as at present. The positive role would be actively to seek to promote the well-being and prosperity of middle-class groups. That some such function is required I have no doubt.

Belgium is one country that has had – since as long ago as 1954 – a Ministry for the Middle Classes. (The present incumbent, M. Louis Olivier, rather delightfully combines this job with the post of Assistant to the Minister for Walloon Affairs (Forestry and Fisheries).) His function is, perhaps, closer to that of a Minister for the Self-Employed, ranging from small tradesmen and professional people to small businesses, which include firms with a staff of up to forty-nine. His main purpose was and is to deal with social security arrangements for the self-employed, with the economic viability of the professions and independent firms, and with professional training. But at the same time as the Ministry was created, the various institutions concerned with the interests of the self-employed and professional classes were given a boost, so that there is now a Conseil Supérieur des Classes Moyennes.

Certainly the creation of such a Ministry would be an immense step forward in this country; small business would for the first time be actively encouraged. But what I am suggesting is something rather wider than this. Even if the general concept is accepted, there is very likely to be a tendency to shy away from the middle-class concept or label, and stick closely to the idea of helping the self-employed. To my mind it is as important for the interests of unorganized labour to be represented at Government level as for those of organized labour.

There is another respect in which Belgian experience is of relevance. The existence of this Ministry did not prevent there being a series of strikes by the self-employed. There were twenty-four-hour strikes in March 1971, October 1972 and most recently on 11 June 1975. Restaurants and cafés were closed, garages shut, taxis unobtainable and most other businesses out of operation. The latest of these strikes resulted in the passage of two bills through the Belgian Parliament. One was specifically to help the self-employed and protect their activities, the other to limit the growth of supermarkets.

As an economic liberal this last is not the sort of legislation that I would welcome in Britain, but it at least indicates the power of this middle-class grouping to force the Belgian Government's hand. Encouraged by this success, the self-employed Belgians are pressing for cuts in their social security contributions and taxes.

This leads naturally to the question, 'Could there be a middle-class strike in this country?' The answer must at present be 'no', but the answer to the question whether doctors would strike would certainly have been 'no' five years ago. To discuss such steps is totally premature in this country. What one can reasonably hope for is that the middle class, under the pressures from which it is suffering, will begin to slough off its diffidence and its reluctance to be strident in its demands. If it does so, then strike action will become simultaneously possible and unnecessary.

I am convinced that this time of maximum pressure on the middle class is also a time of maximum hope. For the first time since the late 1950s there is a prospect that the political pendulum which has seemed to swing towards collectivism, pause, and then swing further left, may be not merely arrested in its movement, but start travelling in the opposite direction. Knowledge is power. Apart from beginning to apply political pressure, the most important thing any member of the middle class can do is to become aware of the processes that have been grinding them down and, above all, of the specific threat of inflation to them, to the country and to democracy. If there is one new organization that it would be supremely worth starting it would be an Anti-Inflation League.

11 A child's guide to political economy

In the last chapter I argued the case for a greater political awareness on the part of the middle class as being the surest means by which it can protect itself. It is, after all, politicians who pass the wrong laws; it is politicians who must be persuaded or induced to pass the right ones. Nothing could be more fatal to the interests either of the middle class or of the country as a whole than the kind of knowing cynicism or weary indifference that refuses to interest itself in the political process. It seems to justify itself on the grounds that politicians are foolish or venal or self-seeking. The danger from a national point of view is that if this is re-iterated often enough it becomes progressively less untrue. The lower the reputation of politics and politicians, the less likely it is that the former will attract the recruits it needs, the more likely that the latter will behave badly.

It is not necessary to go as far as the ancient Greeks who believed that activity in politics was an integral part of every citizen's life. It is sufficient to say that those who do not interest themselves in politics have only themselves to blame when they are hurt by some political action. It is part of the job of politicians to respond to pressures. Most M.P.s indeed are genuinely glad to be presented with a courteous, well-articulated case. The members of the middle class are surely capable of doing this. It does not need grandiose national organizations so much as groups of local citizens to inform and proselytize their M.P.s. This is never a waste of time; even the most sympathetic M.P. may be surprised to find that some idea which he had privately long held, but thought hopeless of achievement in the current climate of opinion had, in fact, behind it an organized body of support.

But if political awareness is important, I am sure that economic awareness is vital. Considering the amount of space and the amount of time that economic topics have commanded in recent years, the degree of ignorance on the subject is astonishing. It is not so much that the wool is pulled over people's eyes as that they tend to pull it over their own by believing things to be true in the public sphere on grounds that they would never accept for a moment if applied to the circumstances of their own lives. It is partly, I think, that economic jargon, the specialist vocabulary that any subject spawns, tends to confuse and overwhelm the public. It is partly that, though economics is – except, perhaps, like all subjects, in its higher reaches – by no means difficult as a topic for study (certainly no more difficult than, say, motor mechanics), many of its conclusions are by no means self-evident. It is almost certainly false, for example, (as I hope to show in a moment) to say that trade unions improve the living standards of their members, or that a better result is achieved by having economic decisions consciously taken in the 'public interest' rather than left to masses of selfish individuals; yet I imagine that if a poll were taken, both these statements would be certified true by the overwhelming mass of the public.

Keynes remarked that economics was a method of thinking rather than a body of settled conclusions. There is no possibility in the space of this chapter of even attempting to give an outline of economic history, economic theory or current economic controversies, such as that between the neo-Keynesians and the monetarists. What there is space for is to concentrate on the area where economics and politics overlap, and to attempt to clear away some of the sheer nonsense which so often surrounds this area.

Let me start with two definitions. As far as economics itself is concerned, there is probably no better definition than the standard one that it is concerned with the allocation of scarce resources. If there were infinite supplies of everything that mankind wanted, from food to energy, there would be no reason to economize, so economics would not be a topic of study and the word 'economics' itself would, no doubt, never have come into use. There were no economists in the Garden of Eden. The advantage of this definition is that it reminds us that economics is about making choices – how can goods best be allocated; it reminds us of the relevance of another old principle – that nothing is for nothing; and it reminds us why economics has been known for so long as the gloomy science. It is very frustrating not to be able to have everything we want, and since economists tend to spend much of their time telling us that if we have more of X we will have to have less of Y, they have never been particularly popular.

The second definition concerns methods of distributing resources. The simplest and most clear-cut division is into two categories, a market economy and a command economy. A market economy is one in which changing relative prices are the main method of allocating resources. Provided the market is a competitive one, the price mechanism enables myriads of consumers to signal their preferences; the firms that are successful in supplying their wants prosper, they attract financial resources in the form of investment, while labour for its part is free to go to the company that will pay the most for its skills.

It is essentially a decentralized system. The alternative is the command economy such as we see in the Soviet Union. Here most, if not all, of the economic decisions are taken centrally – where investment should go, how much of any item should be produced, what its price should be, where workers should be employed and how much they should be paid. In a command economy, the decisions are taken centrally, whether by economic planners or the Politburo. Neither system necessarily need exist in an absolutely pure form. In Britain, for example, we have the nationalized industries, and in addition a number of attempts, from Lord George-Brown on, to formulate national economic plans. In Eastern Europe, on the other hand, there have been a number of attempts to introduce market mechanisms with varying degrees of success into particular areas of the economy.

This leads to the first major fallacy that I want to draw attention to: the notion that decisions taken consciously in the 'public good' are morally superior to, and yield better results than, the 'selfishness'* of private interests competing against each other.

---

* Choice in the market is not in fact based on selfishness but, as Samuel Brittan comments, on 'self-chosen ends', which include scope for philanthropy, family interests, cultural concerns and quality of life. Freedom of choice includes the freedom to 'drop out' if one wishes.

This really deserves a book to itself. To start with, the motives of the disinterested seekers after the public welfare are not necessarily particularly pure. The love of power, the desire for prestige, enjoyment of the trappings of office, a bureaucrat's belief that he really *does* know better – these can be as morally dubious, or more so, than the desire for a quick profit. Next, one must point out that the market place, with millions of consumers voting day by day in favour of this product, against that one, is an intensely democratic one, and a much more accurate method of expressing a preference than a once-in-four-years vote for a package without price-tags that may or may not be carried into practice, and that cannot represent everything the public wants. Finally, one can remark as Ralph Harris[27] has done, that if conscientious planning really did work better than the market, then as we are having more and more planning we would expect the state of the nation to be getting better and better. On the contrary, not only is there less social harmony than ever, but almost every public service is in disarray. The nationalized industries have had and lost £7,000 millions of taxpayers' money since the war, and still no one is very pleased with them, while the Health Service is seething with discontent. In contrast, in the consumer sector there is abundant choice and rising standards in everything from colour television to foreign holidays. It seems that private enterprise is much more responsive to public demand while public enterprise is more responsive to ministerial whim, Government interference and sectional interests.

Before leaving this topic, I must just draw attention to a subsidiary fallacy. It is common form to say that the market would be all right if there were perfect competition, and then point out that there is not. Now it is quite true that the market is imperfect in both the technical sense (which need concern only economists) and the human one. All human institutions are. It therefore functions less efficiently and more expensively than it might in ideal circumstances or indeed than it could if Government intervention did not obstruct competition. But it is quite inadmissible to contrast the market *as it is* with a perfect State system *as it might be*. The State system in practice is not costless or frictionless by any means. Indeed the history of the post-war years suggests that its inefficiency is a good deal higher than that of the private sector.

This leads to the second great fallacy, the notion that the economic system would be much improved if only profit could be minimized or eliminated, the view that profit is at best something distasteful, at worst reprehensible. This is a belief or prejudice that is beginning to crumble under the hard weight of experience. Workers are discovering that when profits vanish their jobs are liable to vanish as well. The Government, for its part, is discovering that when profits vanish so does industrial investment. Reinvested profits enable a firm to expand and modernize, to buy the new plant and machinery that enable it to stay competitive on world markets and produce what the consumer wants at prices he can afford to pay; as for profits distributed in the form of dividends, they either attract fresh capital for the firm distributing them, or are a source of new funds for other firms.

But there is much more to it than this. If there is to be a market economy at all, with freedom of choice for consumers and employees, then profits have an indispensable function as the signal and the measure of success. Their absence is the best possible indication of failure. If the reader doubts this, he has only to look at the British Leyland situation. Profit being absent, the firm collapsed. To keep it in existence and give it some hope of competing with its more successful overseas rivals, the Government is to provide some £1,400 millions over the next few years. Some of this money the Government may succeed in borrowing (which raises problems of its own), but in part at least it will be financed by taxation – in other words compulsory investment by means of a forced levy on the public as a whole. Is this a better way?

At this point I should perhaps add that a market economy has no necessary connection with *laissez-faire*. The State has an important function in regulating the monetary system, protecting the weak, making sure that social costs, such as pollution, are reflected in prices and ensuring that businessmen really *compete*, which they are often notably reluctant to do. Equally, it may wish to see that profits are fairly earned and not the mere result of monopoly situations. In Britain over the past decade, however, the major problem has been too little profit rather than too much, as inflation, taxation and price controls have eaten away at firms' profit margins. Indeed, next to the conquering of inflation, the most urgent single economic task before us is how to switch resources from consumption, whether by the Government or the public, into the company sector to rebuild profitability.

The third great fallacy that would probably command general assent is that trade unions and trade unionism have improved the living standards of trade unionists. (Note that here I am keeping away from the general question of whether trade unions are desirable or undesirable *per se*, and confining myself simply to the economics of it.) Over anything but the shortest possible run, increases in pay come, and can only come out of increases in output and productivity. As Professor Phelps-Brown[28] has pointed out, in 1960 the average wage in the United Kingdom and in Germany would buy about four times as much as that of 1860 had done; in the United States the increase was more than fivefold and in Sweden more than sevenfold. This increase was made possible by a parallel rise in output per worker resulting from more productive equipment and it owed very little to changes in the share of pay relative to profits. There is nowhere else the rise could have come from; real wages depend entirely on the real level of national output, though, as we have seen very clearly in recent years, it is possible for money wages to go up without any improvement in living standards.

It is true that the experience of the last five years might seem to invalidate this general rule. During this time there *has* been a sharp drop in the share of profits relative to wages in the national income. This has been due partly to inflation and partly to price control. It has resulted in lower investment, higher unemployment, and now Government measures designed to reduce everybody's standard of living. To my mind, therefore, this short-term experience reinforces the validity of the long-term general rule.

What then do the trade unions achieve in economic terms? They affect the share of real income that different groups of workers get, that is, they take part in a tug of war with other unions and with non-unionized labour. Since the others tend to catch up after a while, even the effect of this may be relatively short-lived, except where they are able to impose severe restrictions upon entry to the job. They also reduce employment, even when they are protecting it. A less efficient economy means fewer new jobs are created. And, paradoxically, while restrictive practices in specific industries may delay the introduction of labour-saving machinery, they can eventually lead to a position in which only labour-saving measures can enable those industries to survive. A good example of this is the newspaper industry, in which the employers, forced for many years by simple union pressure to employ far more printing workers than were really necessary, now find that only by introducing modern computer-typesetting methods, needing far fewer workers, can they hope to break even.

In all probability trade unions result in the real national income being a good deal lower than it would otherwise have been. They do this in part by preventing the efficient use of new machinery, in part by creating a climate in which the dynamic operation of the whole private sector is quite simply discouraged. Even a small drop – a mere percentage point or two – in the growth of output annually compared to what it would otherwise have been, accumulates over the years to an enormous if unquantifiable figure, which is the amount that members of trade unions are worse off than they would have been if the trade unions did not exist. If this proposition, which I believe to be incontrovertible, proves too hard a bite to swallow, let me present it in a mild and modified form. It is not necessary to postulate the complete absence of trade unions to produce a higher standard of living for all; a different sort of trade unionism, more akin to that found in Germany or the United States of America would have led to a faster increase in total output and thus in total wealth.

Fallacy four also concerns the trade unions. It is the notion that a job once lost is lost for ever. Even people of good will who would like to see high investment and businesses more efficiently run are afraid that if over-manning at our factories lessens then the pool of unemployed will be increased for all time. On the contrary, keeping unneeded workers on in the short term is likely, through making a firm uncompetitive, to lessen employment of prospects in the long term. Moreover, efficient manning levels, if they increase the prosperity of the whole economy, can lead to the formation of new businesses and the expansion of existing ones and thus the creation of new real jobs as opposed to the preservation of pseudo-jobs. Hand weavers were horrified by the prospect of losing their jobs, yet countless more jobs were created subsequently in the textile and machine-making industries than ever existed before. Efficient production makes everyone more prosperous.

None of this is to deny that technological change brings disturbance and may cause hardship, or to minimize in any way the role of the State in protecting displaced workers, retraining or what you will. My argument is that money spent in this way is infinitely more productive than money spent subsidizing pseudo-jobs.

The fifth fallacy is perhaps an easier one to spot than some of its predecessors. It is the notion that if the State pays for a benefit it is free. The only money the State has is what it either borrows or takes from its citizens. All too often a subsidy means simply that someone is made to pay for something he does not want, while somebody who does want it does not pay for it. For example, bus subsidies mean that people who do not use buses pay the fares of those who do. Even a public library (desirable though this may be on other grounds) can best be regarded as a bookshop financed largely by those who do not read books. In general, rather than subsidize, say, the price of bread for everyone, it is economically preferable to put cash in the hands of those who cannot afford to buy bread.

There are so many other elegant and generally accepted beliefs jostling for a place in the catalogue of fallacies, that it is hard to know which to choose. (*Q*: Do statutory minimum wages increase the welfare of the workers concerned? *A*: Yes, if they keep their job. But their main effect is to increase unemployment among people only marginally employable, those whom it would be worth employing at a lower wage. *Q*: What is the effect of import controls? *A*: By banning cheaper foreign goods they increase the cost of living and by keeping resources employed in less efficient parts of the home economy they lower the standard of living.)

The point about subsidies, however, suggests that I should

focus on what is perhaps one of the most striking features of the British economy since the war – our persistent and schizophrenic refusal to give up as much from private consumption as we are demanding by way of public consumption, i.e. our long-term tendency to over-spend. If one ignores the effect of overseas transactions then there are a strictly limited number of ways in which the national income can be distributed. It can be spent by individuals (private consumption), it can be used by companies (private investment), it can be spent by the Government (public consumption), or invested by the Government (public investment). More for one of these must mean less for the others. But because public services are 'free' at the point of consumption, we collectively demand more services (or our representatives demand them on our behalf) than we are individually prepared to give up by way of taxation to finance their supply. When, for example, in 1974 private consumption rose slightly and public consumption shot up, something had to give. It did – in the form of a tremendous drain of cash from the company sector that hurt private investment and could have bankrupted many firms. Moreover, we decline for whatever reason either to take the necessary steps to increase our wealth in line with our spending habits, or to curb our spending in line with our wealth.

In the end, it comes back to choice, and to my remark that nothing is for nothing. Economics is a method of helping people to choose between various ways of disposing of resources and of assessing the various costs and benefits involved. It does not, and it never has, enabled the laws of common sense, logic or arithmetic to be suspended, though too many people act as if it does. Knowledge is power, and since the middle class needs all the power it can muster in the coming years, I would urge its members to take more rather than less interest in economic affairs. But if they start from the few principles expounded here, they are less likely to be deceived.

12 How to save your school

All the evidence suggests that middle-class protest is most likely to be effective when directed towards specific objectives, for a specific purpose. One of the most important fields in which the weight of middle-class opinion can make itself felt is that of education, and no one who has persevered with me so far is likely to be deterred by the accusation that they are putting forward 'a middle-class point of view' or forming 'a middle-class protest group'. Indeed, they are, and what is wrong with that?

It is quite true that the middle class has a vested interest in education, and is often accused of deriving an unfair advantage from the educational system. Raynor writes, 'Their privileged position in education is almost absolute. Numerous pieces of research both private and governmental have demonstrated the clear advantages enjoyed by the middle class.' However, he gives the game away a little later when he adds: 'Not only do they show greater interest in the child's education, they afford them the benefits of pre-school education in nursery schools and play groups . . . the school and the home pull in similar ways, sharing similar values and attitudes.'[29]

This, of course, is the nub of the matter. A child whose parents care passionately about education, from a home in which books are as much part of the furniture as a television set, in which, from an early age, it is stimulated by conversation employing a relatively large vocabulary, in which much store is set on intellectual achievement, a child who is read to, taken on visits and foreign travel, a child from such a background is going to have an immense advantage over one from a home where there is ignorance and indifference. I am not suggesting that this idealized picture universally applies among the middle class, rather that there is no reason whatever to feel guilty about caring about one's children's education. In my view, the middle-class parent who cares about good schooling is performing a positive service to the whole community. Indeed, perhaps the only strong argument in favour of the abolition of private education is the impetus that such a move would give to the improvement of the State system.

There are two specific areas in education in which middle-class interests are at stake. They concern quality of education and choice of type. On the question of quality of education, there is little need of advice from me. The problem has arisen from a straightforward confusion as to educational goals. There is, inevitably, a clash between the highest possible excellence and the maximum possible equality, and depending on which of these goals is put first, the shape of the educational system will vary. Many educationalists, and still more sociologists, put the drive towards equality first. *Their* ideal educational system will have room for as much excellence as is compatible with equality. An achievement-oriented system will have as much equality as is compatible with excellence. One point of view is quite prepared to see less rigorous intellectual standards, with the best pupils attaining less, provided the less gifted achieve more. In its extreme expression, this takes the form of being prepared to bus bright children to slum schools, to their enormous personal disadvantage, in order to improve, in the long term, the character of the school and its educational 'mix'. No parents concerned for their child's interests should be prepared to tolerate such a policy and there is no reason why they should feel under any moral compulsion to do so. A lowering of standards can only, in the long run, disadvantage those whom it is intended to help.

The nearest analogy here is the concept of liberty; this is not merely a luxury but a real need. It is sometimes suggested that liberty is worthless because it cannot be enjoyed, say, by the starving. On the contrary, those who enjoy liberty hold it, not just for themselves, but in trust for those who do not yet possess it. They would be guilty of an unpardonable breach of trust not to fight for it. In the same way educational excellence and the maintenance of standards of scholarship are among the most priceless achievements of civilization; there is nothing to be said for watering them down.

We can, therefore, look with grave suspicion upon any proposals which equate educational advance with a lowering of standards. In addition, middle-class parents, since they believe – as do many other parents – that standards of morality, of behaviour, of courtesy and of speech are important, will be naturally concerned that these things should be inculcated by the schools, and that their children should not attend schools where they are neglected, brutalized or subjected to precocious sexual initiation. In this they are no different from other parents – merely more articulate. But while there is a choice of schools the concerned parent educating his children within the State system is usually able to find one whose methods are nearer rather than further away from his standards. There is always the possibility of moving to an area with a more suitable school. Indeed one definition of a middle-class parent might well be 'somebody prepared to uproot himself for the sake of his children's education'. If he prefers private education, then the immediate enemy is inflation. If that is not controlled everything goes. There is a longer-term danger – that there might be an eventual attempt to make education a State monopoly. If that were ever seriously proposed, it would have to be fought to the death, but so far it is no more than a gleam in some extreme socialists' eyes. This is a book about immediate dangers – there are more than enough of those.

The immediate danger as far as education and the middle class is concerned is of total enforced comprehensivization. To say this is not to attack the idea of comprehensive schools as such: some are good, some are bad, some are indifferent. It *is* to attack the totalitarian notion that no single school can truly be called comprehensive while any other school of a different type exists offering a choice. It must be a curious form of education that can only flourish if every other type is destroyed. My own view, for what it is worth, is that nobody knows what the best form of education is. It must thus be desirable to have as many different sorts of school as possible. We say, in fact, with Mao Tse-tung, 'Let a hundred flowers bloom.' To this, we can add two further points. First, that though the quality of any school depends to some large measure on the quality of the head teacher and all great schools demand a great head teacher, genius is a quality in short supply. A competent head teacher can run a competent grammar school, but the extremes of progressive education require enormous gifts of character for their success. A. S. Neill, by any standards a very remarkable man, was able to run a worthwhile school on completely libertarian principles. The history of the William Tyndale School in Islington, subject to parents' protests, a drastic falling-off in numbers and, finally, a public inquiry, shows what is liable to happen to unstructured education in less capable hands.

Second, we can say that very good schools do not emerge overnight. There is no formula for their creation; at the least, years of dedicated work are required. If good schools exist, they should be cherished; for any single one to be wantonly destroyed seems the height of folly. The move towards comprehensive education has already gone a long way in this country. This means we have reached the point at which, if it is to become universal, then the remaining maintained grammar schools must vanish. This is the point at which many parents will want to resist, particularly since sufficient time has elapsed for the problems of comprehensive schools, particularly of large, urban comprehensives, to become apparent.

What can be done in these circumstances? The answer is 'A good deal' for the simple reason that, as the law stands, neither the Government nor the Secretary of State for Education has any power to enforce the closure of grammar or other selective schools upon the local education authorities. This goes to the heart of the organization of education in Britain. The British system is not one in which the central government is responsible for the organization of education and in a position to impose its policy universally. To quote two leading authorities:

The British educational system . . . has long consisted of a diarchy between the Secretary of State and the local education authorities. Each has a vital part to play, with separate rights and duties. Such a system is far more responsive to local needs than a State-centred one; its ideal is a harmonious co-operation between the local authorities and the Secretary of State, as free as possible from any attempt on the part of central government to dictate to the local educational authorities on political grounds.[30]

Thus, when the then Secretary of State for Education, Mr Reg Prentice, sent out the notorious circular 4/74 to local education authorities demanding by a specified date 'a statement of final intent' regarding their plans for reorganizing secondary education, there was a strong element of bluff in his move. A number of local authorities kow-towed to this demand. Others, however, notably Buckinghamshire (which has a partly comprehensive system) and Bexley, returned a dusty answer. This was within their rights, since while the circular sets out the Government's policy and seeks, as such documents have long done, to persuade those concerned to adopt it, such circulars do not have any legal force. Other authorities preferred to adopt delaying tactics, agreeing to the demand to go completely comprehensive as and when adequate finance was available or at some distant date in the future.

Mr Prentice then responded with a mixture of bluster and bullying, saying in effect that the Government was sovereign (which, as we have seen in educational matters, is not true) and intended to compel the recalcitrant authorities to comply.

There were two possible methods open to the Government to seek compliance. The first, which was indicated in the circular, was to seek to withhold finance for future building programmes. It is extremely doubtful, in fact, how far it can go, or, indeed, how effective this sanction could be. It is the duty of the Secretary of State under S.1 of the 1944 Act to promote the education of the people of England and Wales and the progressive development of institutions devoted to that purpose and to produce the effective execution by local authorities of the national policy for the providing of a varied and comprehensive (in the true sense of the word) educational service in every area. The local authority in turn has a duty to provide and equip schools, and to secure that the premises of every school maintained by them conform to the standards prescribed by the Secretary of State.

The cumulative effect of these provisions seems to be such that, if the Secretary of State tried to apply financial sanctions which prevented the adequate maintenance of the existing buildings, or their necessary repair or alteration, there would at the very least be a possibility of seeking legal redress. In the words of St John-Stevas and Brittan, 'There is a reasonable chance that the Courts would intervene on the basis that such action was contrary to the policy of the 1944 Act which has to be looked at as a whole.'

The Education Minister would seem to be on safer ground if he merely refused to sanction the building of any new schools, or significant enlargements of existing ones unless they were part of a plan to go comprehensive. This is clearly what Mr Prentice had in mind when he said in his notorious 4/74 circular: 'He does not propose to include in future building programmes projects of non-comprehensive schools, whether grammar, technical or modern, except when such projects are necessary to enable the schools to become comprehensive.' Here it is up to local education authorities to be artful. The key point is to propose only alterations that are compatible with a fully comprehensive system; if these are turned down then the Secretary of State himself is blocking progress in the direction he desires, and this he is unlikely to do.

The alternative open to the Government was to pass a Bill through Parliament seeking to enforce a fully comprehensive system, and this they duly decided to do. On 18 December 1975 the Government published an eight-clause Bill designed to force local authorities to introduce wholly comprehensive education whether they liked it or not. It also removed the independence guaranteed to voluntary schools, and gave the Government veto powers over local authority places at independent schools. After a bitter Parliamentary battle the Bill finally received the Royal Assent and passed into law on 22 November 1976.

What the Act does, or purports to do, is to require local education authorities 'to have regard to the "comprehensive principle"'. It gives the Secretary of State for Education and Science power to require authorities to submit proposals for the re-organization of their schools on comprehensive lines, either for the whole of their area or for particular districts. If the proposals could be implemented within five years and are not obviously unacceptable, then she (Mrs Shirley Williams, the present

Education Minister) will direct that they should be subject to the normal Section 13 procedure under the 1944 Education Act – of which more anon – and then if they are approved the proposers are required to implement them. If, however, the proposals are unacceptable to the Secretary of State, then she may refer them back and call for further proposals from the local education authority. She also has the power to require proposals from the governors of voluntary schools, that is, schools publicly maintained but established in most cases by the Churches and other charitable foundations.

At first reading this may well sound sad. In fact, however, there is no reason whatever why the seven local education authorities who ostentatiously defied the Minister, or the thirty others who declared themselves unable to offer definite plans for going completely comprehensive by a firm date, should feel the slightest whit abashed. Provided they keep their nerve, and provided they are backed by parents in the area, there is no reason at all why they should not continue to hold out, at least until the electorate in another general election have had the opportunity to pass judgement on this revolutionary new Act.

Delay is still a potent tactic, particularly at a time when funds are going to be in short supply for any sort of major building programme. One thinks with admiration of the resistance to the various schemes to build a relief road through Christ Church meadow in Oxford. For year after year after year, the matter dragged on, with fresh inquiries, fresh debates, fresh protests. At the very last of the inquiries Professor Colin Buchanan came forward and with the weight of his authority as a traffic expert said that the whole scheme was a nonsense. At the time the delays had seemed highly inefficient, but if any prompter decision had been taken it would have been the wrong one for the simple reason that Buchanan-type expertise had not been in existence earlier to demolish the case. As it was, delay was the most efficient policy.

The point is a simple one. It is the duty of the local authority to operate as efficiently and as conscientiously as it can. Although the Minister has acted very promptly in demanding that the recalcitrant authorities should submit schemes to her, these cannot be drawn up overnight. There is no question of defying the law. A local authority which seeks to do its duty cannot be satisfied, merely because the Act orders it to 'have regard' to the principle of comprehensive education, to produce a botched or inefficient scheme. It is all too likely to find, in these days of financial stringency, that it quite simply lacks the resources to make even a half-way decent scheme viable. On it rests the responsibility for the children in its area; there is no timetable in the new Act and the relationship between its provisions and the great principles laid down in the 1944 Act may yet have to be decided in the courts.

Some eminent legal authorities indeed think that the Act has been so sloppily drawn up that it may prove to be a virtual dead letter. In particular, its insistence on the comprehensive principle being applied universally seems in stark conflict with the key principle of the 1944 Act that as far as practicable children shall be educated in accordance with the wishes of their parents. This section of the 1944 Act has not been repealed, and only the courts can decide where the new Act stands in the light of it.

Some education officials take the view that parental choice now no longer exists. In the words of a draft circular from the Department of Education and Science:

Questions of a school's suitability to the aptitude and ability of a child are not expected to remain of practical significance for much longer, as they should not normally arise in the case of admissions to a comprehensive school.

It may take the courts to test this one too. In considering legal action local authorities and all who care about their children's education can be enormously heartened by the implications of the Tameside judgment in August 1976. Tameside swung from Labour to Conservative in the May 1976 local elections, and at once scrapped a hastily prepared plan for going comprehensive. The Education Minister sought to compel the council to press ahead with the abolition of its grammar schools, but the House of Lords, as the final court of appeal, found in favour of the council. It ruled that the Minister could not substitute his own view for that of the education authority, provided that the education authority had acted reasonably.

This important judgment means that if a Minister wants to intervene under Section 68 of the Education Act, it is not enough merely for him to *believe* that a local authority is acting unreasonably. He has to *prove* it. This is a severe restriction on what was previously thought to be the Minister's power.

Even if one despairs and assumes – which I do not for a moment believe – the destruction of the remaining grammar schools, it would be wrong to think of this as an example of irreversible change. Changes can be irreversible in the sense that nobody wishes to reverse them, but provided there is the political will all other changes can be reversed. I see no reason why a future, less doctrinaire Government should not restore to local authorities the right – should they so wish – to start new schools on the lines of those that will have been lost.

In the meantime there is the question of what to do if one is a parent anxious to help preserve an existing school. Let me start with the maintained county grammar schools, which are the selective secondary schools provided and fully maintained by the local education authority. The parents can help a great deal. The local authority has to give public notice of its proposals, and any ten or more local government electors can, within two months, submit objections to the Secretary of State. Obviously, the more broadly based the objections the better; the ideal combination is obviously that of parents, teachers, governors, ex-pupils, any councillors in disagreement with the majority and electors from any or all parties.

The Secretary of State has power to order a local inquiry before deciding on the proposals, though unfortunately he cannot be compelled to do so. However, the wider the protest the better the chance of an inquiry. The Secretary of State also has the power to modify proposals submitted to him before approving them, but this power is circumscribed; he cannot modify them to the extent that they become a new and different proposal, and if he did this can be challenged in the courts.

All this may seem no more than delaying action but as I have said before, never, ever underestimate the importance of delay. Certainly, if the local authority seeks to change the character of the school in an indirect way, that is without making a so-called

Section 13 proposal, then the parents are on strong grounds. Significant changes can only be made via one of the Section 13 proposals to which I referred. Thus, if a local authority has a selective school in its area it is bound to provide a genuine selection procedure, as otherwise it is altering the character of the school in a significant respect. As the then Secretary of State said in Parliament in 1972, 'Until proposals for changes of character of existing schools have been approved, local education authorities have a responsibility to operate them without such changes.'

This is not the place to discuss in any detail the position of the voluntary schools, either voluntary-aided or voluntary-controlled. Those concerned can find a full discussion in *How to Save Your Schools*, the pamphlet by Norman St John-Stevas and Leon Brittan I have already quoted from. As far as voluntary-aided schools are concerned, the local authority appoints only one third of the governors, the others being independently appointed by the voluntary body. The only people who can make a significant change in the character of the school are the governors themselves. If they stand out against the local education authority then the only sanction the latter has is to seek to withdraw financial assistance from the school. This would require a Section 13 application – with the same opportunities for objection – and what is more the authority would have to be able to provide places for the children attending the voluntary school if it ceased to be available to the authority. Perhaps the most important point for voluntary-aided school governors is that they have the right to put forward objections to any proposals by the local authority to establish or maintain a *new* school. The importance of this is that they should be alert to object to the establishment of new school places which might later on render their own school redundant.

As for voluntary-controlled schools, these are much less independent, with two thirds of the governors appointed by the local education authority. Even here, however, if the governors, even the local-authority-appointed ones, decline to put forward proposals for reorganization, then the only way the authority can impose its will is by dismissing them and appointing more compliant individuals. It is worth pointing out that under the

new Act the Secretary of State cannot approve Section 13 proposals for the significant enlargement of a voluntary-aided school
whose governors satisfy her that they are unable to pay their
share (15 per cent) of the capital cost of the enlargement.

There remains the question of the direct grant schools, those
independent grammar schools which make a proportion of their
places available to the local authority and, as a result, receive a
direct grant from the Government. Here, for the present, nothing
can be done to prevent the Government phasing out this support.
The result will be that up to a hundred of these schools are becoming wholly fee-paying, to the obvious detriment of able children whose parents cannot pay the fees.

Under the Education Acts of 1944 and 1953 local authorities
had the right to take up places at these schools. The 1976 Act
gives the Secretary of State the power to revoke any general
approval for arrangements made for taking up places, and requires authorities to seek her approval for continuing or initiat-
ing these arrangements in future.

From some points of view this is the worst provision in the
Act. These places are of enormous value, especially for parents of
modest means. They also save considerable sums of money. The
fees qualify for rate-support grant, and the local authority itself
saves the capital expenditure which would be needed to provide
new school places. It is up to local authorities to stick to their
guns and see how far the Minister is prepared to go in taking on
herself the odium of overruling their wishes.

The next general election must be held by October 1979 at the
latest. Few Parliaments go their full term, and given the economic situation many of us would expect it to come a good deal
sooner than that. There is thus a considerable opportunity of
keeping the options open till the electorate has spoken once more,
and that by wholly legal means. Even in matters of education
there is evidence that the tide is beginning to turn. 'Abolish the
eleven-plus' has been a powerful slogan. A point is being reached
at which 'Must all schools be the same?' begins to have an impact. Children's needs *differ*; of my two eldest daughters, one is
at a local comprehensive, the other a voluntary-controlled grammar school, and I have no doubt that the education that suits one

would be quite unsuitable for the other. Indeed, Buckingham-shire, the county in which I happen to live, provides an interesting example of the demand by parents for the possibility of grammar school education. Part of the county is entirely comprehensive; the other part retains grammar schools. This is, perhaps, an unstable situation. Certainly, it has been found necessary to erect an invisible fence right across the county, cutting off parents in one half from the education available in the other. This is not, as you might think, to prevent them flooding the comprehensive schools. It is to stop those in the comprehensive part of the county from flooding the grammar schools. Parents care about education, and parents of all social classes are to be found selling their homes and moving house across the barrier. How did I, living 400 yards the wrong side of the fence, manage to jump it for one child? First – and again this is very important for the middle-class parent – by being able to put up a very special case. Second, by two years' hard work and tenacity.

Before leaving the subject of education, let me mention one possibility that could, in the long run, render these agonizing controversies wholly redundant. This possibility is the provision of educational vouchers entitling the parent to a given quantum of education. This they would be entitled to exchange *at the school of their choice* at which they would enrol their child. The main object of such a scheme is to give effect to the general principle enshrined in the 1944 Act and already referred to, under which 'so far as is compatible with the provision of efficient training and the avoidance of expenditure pupils are to be educated in accordance with the wishes of their parents'. For the first time parent power could make itself effectively felt. The belief is that schools to which parents chose not to send their children would fairly rapidly change or be changed – though in fairness the William Tyndale precedent in Islington is not an encouraging one.

The flexibility of such schemes is potentially endless. It would be possible to give parents of disadvantaged children vouchers of higher value, thereby exercising the healthiest form of positive discrimination. The vouchers could be redeemable only in local authority schools, or if desired could be encashed at any approved educational establishment, and so on. There is a pressure group called Fever (Friends of the Education Voucher Experiment in Representative Regions). The title is significant, since nobody is suggesting that this is a change which could or should be made overnight. Instead in carefully selected areas (Kent is one of the likeliest) an experiment could be put under way to see how it works in practice. It is worth noting that these proposals are beginning to arouse intense alarm, both on the left and among some teachers. The teachers, in particular the National Union of Teachers, are alarmed at the thought that they might become directly answerable to parents. As for the left, having called for years for power to the people, it is agonizing at the prospect that the people might use that power in ways it did not much care for. The Education Correspondent of the *New Statesman* even went so far as to suggest that educational decisions might be too important for parents to be trusted with them. Since Fever is merely calling for experiments with the system, it is a call that is becoming very hard to resist. Parents interested will find it worth reading *Experiment with Choice in Education* by Alan Maynard (Institute of Economic Affairs, 2 Lord North Street, London, SW1, £1). This outlines no less than eight different possible voucher schemes, showing, if nothing else, how flexible such a means of registering parental preferences might be.

In the last resort, in education as in anything else, it is the mobilization of public opinion that counts. Whether in seeking to protect an existing school or in pioneering a new system of educational finance, it is up to like-minded parents and citizens not to be afraid of banding together and creating an effective muscle-power that can be used both to make propaganda for their cause and to make the lives of the illiberal and the obscurantists as much of a misery as possible.

13 How to scare your council

The title of this chapter is perhaps the only note of over-optimism
I have allowed myself in this book; councils do not scare easily.
There is no bureaucracy like a council bureaucracy, and indeed I
can think of two examples that well illustrate the rock-like resistance that the ordinary citizen can encounter. The first occurred
some years ago, when I was living in Barnsbury in the London
Borough of Islington. A largely middle-class section of the local
residents had formed an association to put pressure on the local
council to effect environmental improvements in the neighbourhood. (This was the time when concern about the environment
was just beginning to spread and when the argument about
demolition versus rehabilitation as applied to old houses was
beginning to catch fire.) The Barnsbury Association strongly
opposed the Council's plan to demolish some nineteenth-century
housing to build new blocks of flats and put up a strong case at
the Public Inquiry that was held. The then Minister of Housing
let the Council's plan go through, but was sufficiently impressed
by the Association's case to command an Environmental Scheme
to be drawn up for Barnsbury, naturally under the aegis of the
Council. A team of experts got to work to study the neighbourhood and draw up a report. However, it was impossible to suggest methods of improvement and future policies without imply-
ing criticisms of some existing Council policies. That is where the
trouble started. The members of the town planning team began
to get increasingly unhappy as they felt themselves under pressure, and their unhappiness turned to fury when their draft
report, was, to some extent, bowdlerized by the Council's officials,
that is to say, every word of implied criticism cut out. As a result
of this, a copy of the uncensored Draft Report fell into my hands

and I was able to compare this with the Report as published. I wrote an article in the *Spectator* comparing the two.

The reaction of the Council was remarkable. It blandly denied that the Draft Report existed and nothing was able to shake it from this attitude. Thus no question of censorship arose. When I issued a series of public challenges, it wisely declined to take them up. There was a complete blank wall. Obviously I had one hand tied behind my back in the sense that I could not reveal my sources, but to be able to get nowhere was frustrating in the extreme. Months later it happened that a delegation from the Barnsbury Association went to see the then Minister, Mr Anthony Greenwood. In the course of the conversation, one of his junior ministers, Mr Fred Willey, admitted to me in an undertone that he (Mr Willey) had seen the famous and disputed draft. What depressed me at the time was that, as a journalist, I was in a much stronger position than ordinary members of the public. I could publicize our case. If I could get nowhere, I thought at the time, what hope was there for ordinary members of the public?

The second example concerns the Council at Bletchley in Buckinghamshire, near where I now live. In the years preceding the reorganization of local government, the Council had drawn up plans to build a so-called leisure pool, that is, a relatively shallow swimming pool of irregular shape, in a setting which included, improbably for Bletchley, palm trees. So far, possibly, so good. Unfortunately the scheme involved the demolition of the existing old-fashioned and untrendy pool, which was much used by swimming clubs and to teach children swimming. The new pool was quite unsuitable for any competitive purposes. There was very strong local opposition which grew to a crescendo when the Swimming Club discovered that the alternative facilities it had been offered at a local school were more restricted and much, much more expensive than it had been promised. There was agitation, protests, attempts to get an injunction, and a councillor particularly associated with the scheme was defeated the next time he stood. All in vain. These schemes acquire a life of their own and, in spite of the fact that the Council was about to cease to exist under the reorganization, demolition of the old pool went ahead.

I start with these two adverse examples because it is important to realize what one is up against. In theory a council, because it is local, should be more responsive to pressure than a national body. In practice, many councils tend to be more secretive, more self-satisfied, more bureaucratic (because the bureaucracy is of a lower calibre) and even less accountable than other public bodies. It can be harder to make them retreat, if only because the lower the relative calibre of an organization or an individual, the less ready it is to admit a mistake and the more likely simply to dig its heels in.

However, it is the limited nature of a local bureaucracy that makes it ultimately vulnerable. The individual seeking the redress of a grievance has to overcome any compunction, or any dislike of making himself a nuisance. Officials, all officials, like a quiet life. He has to resolve they shall not get it. If a decision is taken, usually by a council official, that adversely affects you, the aim is obviously to get it reversed as quickly as possible. The first rule is that there is a much better chance of getting someone to change his mind if the argument is in private. Initially one is seeking to avoid a situation in which his prestige or self-esteem is involved; if one can avoid it, there is a much better chance of a satisfactory outcome. Stage One therefore is polite, well-reasoned letters and/or telephone calls to the official concerned. I favour a direct approach, provided you know what you are doing, rather than through your councillor, because once somebody else is negotiating on your behalf, control of the negotiations is out of your hands. Only if one gets no satisfaction does the dispute escalate. Stage Two involves briefing the councillor for your particular area; at Stage Three you approach your Member of Parliament (whether or not he belongs to your party) because he can often carry considerable clout in local affairs. Stage Four involves using the second most powerful weapon you have – publicity. Local newspapers are always avid for local news stories, and provided you brief the reporter carefully, you will have no reason to complain of the coverage. This is the time to involve any local bodies available, Ratepayers' Associations, the local Chamber of Commerce, the political parties if appropriate. The most powerful weapon you have against the entrenched and the unsackable is the weapon of ridicule. If you can now use it, do so, because so often the type of decision the local citizen is protesting against is one that flies against all reason, whether it is small like the siting of a private driveway, failure to impose a speed limit, or large like some grandiose spending plan. (In the latter connection never let council officials get away with the argument that it is important to spend the money now, because the project will cost twice as much in a few years' time. If it cannot be afforded, it cannot be afforded now. If it is an economically viable project, it will still be economically viable five years from now.) National newspapers which love a good, local scandal, can often be drawn in, while the B.B.C.'s consumer programme Checkpoint can provide a very valuable outlet for legitimate grievances. Don't hesitate to use all five stages, but never forget that it is much, much better to win at Stage One.*

So far we have been discussing getting individually bad decisions reversed. There is no running away from the fact, however, that it is the level and incidence of rates that provides the main middle-class complaint against councils. Income tax at least goes down if your income does. In the last resort you can use less electricity if its price goes up beyond all reason. But the rise in rates – one third or more in 1975–6, another 10 per cent or more in 1976–7 – goes remorselessly on.

The main objection is a well-established one. Approximately two thirds of local government expenditure is paid for out of central government funds, while one third is paid for out of rates, which are a simple property tax. There are some 25 million taxpayers but only 16 million ratepayers, which suggests that a large number of people are not, in fact, paying for the local services which they enjoy. Moreover, rates are levied according to the value of the property alone. The extreme cases are an elderly couple living in the house they have occupied all their married lives but now enjoying a relatively low income (who may or may not qualify for a rates rebate) and a family consisting of several wage- or salary-earners occupying a low-rated house.

* In cases of injustice caused by specific administrative default the Commissioner for Local Administration can be drawn in, but it is not very often that this can be proved. But at least there is now a local Ombudsman.

When rates were relatively low this anomaly seemed endurable, but the escalation of rates – an average rise of 390 per cent since 1960 – has understandably led to enormous bad feeling. The long-established National Union of Ratepayers' Associations, solemn in its outlook and dignified in its protests, suddenly found itself sharing the stage with the National Association of Ratepayers' Action Groups, which sprang up quasi-spontaneously as the size of the 1974 rate increases began to sink in. N.A.R.A.G., the newer body, seemed prepared to flirt with direct or extra-legal action, such as withholding rate payments.

Again, the issue came first, and then the organization, but the flood-tide of protest – at a time when a minority Government was in office and approaching an inevitable election – certainly had the effect of persuading the Secretary of State to add £140 millions to the Rate Support Grant in the late summer of 1974. Before considering long-term solutions to the rates problem, however, it is worth considering why they have soared in recent years.

The first reason is inflation. It is a fact that local government services, like those of the central government, are very labour-intensive. Rises in costs in manufacturing industry are, to some extent, offset by increases in productivity – better machines more efficiently manned. There is virtually no increase in productivity inside the Government and local government machine. This means that the cost of these services rises faster than the overall rise in the cost of living. Of course, to say that inflation is a reason is not to use it – as many councils will – as an excuse.

Next there is the local government reorganization introduced by Mr Peter Walker, who was Secretary of State for the Environment in Mr Heath's Administration. This introduced a two-tier system of local government, with new district councils covering much larger areas than previously. One of the few almost wholly non-controversial statements it is possible to make in party politics is that the reorganization was a financial disaster, and it is very hard to find anyone in any party with a good word to say for it now. The reorganization was expensive in itself, and there is no possible doubt that it provided a splendid opportunity for empire-building on a large scale. Relatively modestly paid council officials seized the opportunity to take much-better-paid jobs with the new authorities, which they themselves were involved in setting up. Their wider responsibilities naturally required them to have more staff, also better paid than hitherto (since they, too, were promoted). Those few who did not make the switch had to be expensively compensated, and so on.

The third reason, and one to which the councils themselves will always point, is the wider range of duties put upon them by central government. It is certainly true that roughly two thirds of local expenditure goes on education, and the salaries of teachers, for example, have leapt upwards in recent years.

Above all, however, there is the harsh fact that – except for the pressure of irate ratepayers at election time – there is virtually no incentive whatsoever on any council employee to cut costs. There are certainly no financial rewards for doing so; indeed all that a determinedly cost-conscious official would achieve would be a smaller department than in other comparable authorities, fewer staff under him, less prestige. Indeed, in America their ever-ingenious economists have developed a whole 'economic theory of bureaucracy'. This suggests that just as a company director tries to maximize profits, or a sales director his sales, so public officials obtain their main satisfaction from maximizing the rate of growth of their 'bureaux'.

Whatever the reasons, there is no doubt that there has been, over the past decade, a very large increase in the number of people employed by local authorities. Between June 1964 and June 1974 the total rose by just over 800,000, from just over 2 millions to 2·83 millions. Central Government staff rose from 1,350,000 in 1964 to 1,750,000 in 1975, and there seems to have been a further rise in both national and local staffs in the first half of 1975. By way of comparison, employment in the private sector fell by 1 million between 1964 and 1974.

It may be argued that some of this increase comes from rising standards of social services, but how much comes from the bureaucracies that manage those social services?

It is this apparently remorseless rise in the cost of local government that has led to strong demands for cash limits, that is, a cash ceiling on council spending, adjusted perhaps for the fall in the value of money, but certainly not specially adjusted for the additional cost of council projects, which, as I have pointed out, often inflate much more rapidly than costs as a whole. Such a system is highly desirable, and at the time of writing the Government is groping its way towards limiting the rise in local spending by limiting the central Government grant towards local government services.

There are, however, snags of which militant ratepayers should be aware. The first is that bureaucracies, especially perhaps benevolent bureaucracies, have a life of their own. Any council official worth his salt is a past master at finding good reasons why cuts are impossible. The most frequently used dodge, when asked for a list of possible economies, is to produce a list of highly popular services to be slashed. Cut the mobile libraries, or close the small village schools, the officials helpfully suggest. When protests are made they promptly reply: 'Well, that shows how impossible it is to make economies.'

The other snag can be still more difficult to overcome. Take education as an example. The public may not like paying rates, but in their role as parents they want the best possible schools, and rightly. It is therefore all too easy to muster public protests against any suggestions for cuts. In my own county of Buckinghamshire, the County Council was appalled to find that its education budget was due to rise by more than 50 per cent in 1975. It therefore proposed to trim a few percentage points off the rise. That most articulate of pressure groups, the National Union of Teachers, had no difficulty in organizing protests. There were petitions, demonstrations, sit-downs in the market square outside the County Offices – all in protest against 'savage cuts' in education. Useless to point out that a rise in educational spending of around 50 per cent could hardly be described as a savage cut, and that all that was being trimmed was the size of the increase. In the end a compromise was reached. There were some economies, but the cuts themselves were trimmed down. It will be interesting to see when the 1976 County Budget is discussed whether public opinion has moved and the facts of the crisis have sunk in.*

*They seem to have – at least with the public. In spite of a programme of cuts, the ruling party increased its majority in the 1977 local elections.

In fact, local government spending needs to be attacked from many angles. There need to be rigid cash limits on spending – any family (and what is a council but an extended family?) finds that in inflationary times it has to abandon hopes of holidays or purchases it would have liked to make, and it is insane for public authorities to be exempt from such disciplines.

There needs to be a reduction in manning levels – even a 2 per cent reduction year by year in staff would be a great advance. We have to get across the revolutionary notion that there should be a real choice between employing, say, twenty people at £4,000 a year or ten people at £8,000. And the situation in which architects, for example, are deserting the private sector to take much-better-paid council jobs needs to be ended. It is, in my view, more important to cut staff levels than capital projects – otherwise the project is axed, but somehow the staff remains the same.

We must try – and it is no good underestimating the difficulties – to get a change of attitude on cost-saving – giving bonuses perhaps for thrift. And we should at least experiment with employing outside contractors to perform some services – refuse collection, for example.

All this leaves open the question of rates. Change is in the air and there is a committee examining the question of local government finance. N.A.R.A.G. wants local government financed quite simply from national Income Tax. The National Union of Ratepayers' Associations wants national services, such as education, financed nationally, but, in addition, a local income tax to pay for local services. Though paying for local government will never be painless a different system might be a good deal fairer.

In the last analysis what is required is informed rather than merely inflamed local opinion. It is not enough merely to be angry about the rates – reasonable though this reaction may be. Such agitations inevitably die down. What is needed is an understanding of the processes whereby local government spending rises, and the drawing of a clear distinction between the provision of better services and the operation of a non-cost-conscious bureaucracy. In America electors are often asked to vote to authorize the issue of bonds for some specific municipal project, and there is much to be said for introducing much more participation in local decision-making. In particular there is everything to be said for inviting ratepayers, by means of local polls, to choose between differing levels of expenditure and services. I can think of a number of councils that would be scared stiff at any such suggestion, so perhaps the title of this chapter is justified after all.

14 An attitude to tax

When this book was first conceived, one of its main purposes was to provide as much practical advice as possible, since this is an exceptionally difficult time for the middle class. As the material developed, two things became clear. The first was, as I have not hesitated to repeat, that the most practical thing the middle class could do was to understand the roots of its predicament, and resolve to apply all possible counter-pressures. The second was that most people need specific advice, tailored to their particular circumstances. (Only a minority, fortunately, are as apocalyptic as a friend who, when I asked him what he would really like to learn from a book such as this, replied: 'How to board up the windows and erect a barbed-wire barricade.') The diversity of activities that helps to prevent the middle class combining means that its individual problems are as diverse as its interests.

In no field is this truer than that of taxation, where it is rare to find two individuals in exactly the same circumstances. All the same, it is undoubtedly true that a very large number of people pay more tax than they need to, or at the very least do not arrange their affairs to take account of what their taxation position is. To give a simple example of this, there are very many people with money in a building society for whom a building society is not the best form of investment. This is because building society interest is paid free of tax or 'tax paid'. The actual net rate of interest paid is not particularly high, but it is not liable to income tax for standard rate payers, and such people would thus have to obtain a very high rate of interest before tax, in order to be left with what the building society gives them. But, if they do not have to pay income tax, for the reason that their total income is simply not big enough, then they can do better by putting their savings, for example, in suitable gilt-edged securities or local authority loans.

This may seem a small enough instance, but I know from my postbag that it is a very common one. What is even more surprising is the number of people who do not claim all the tax allowances lawfully due to them, ranging from a claim for a dependent relative to the appropriate relief on insurance premium payments.

The first and most important rule, therefore, is that there is no moral virtue in paying more tax than you absolutely must. It was a great judge, Lord Clyde, who as long ago as 1920 put the matter as robustly as it is ever likely to be expressed. 'No man in this country is under the smallest obligation, moral or other, so to arrange his affairs as to enable the Inland Revenue to put the largest possible shovel into his stores.' This was true then. It is more than ever true today; with Governments spending your money like a drunken sailor, it is hard for even the most sanctimonious citizen to take much joy or comfort in handing over to the Inland Revenue more money than he is strictly and absolutely compelled to. You will note that I am not suggesting fraud, dishonesty or evasion; simply that if you pay more tax than you have to, then you are doing yourself harm and nobody else any good. If you feel an absolute compulsion to make an altruistic gesture, you would do much better to burn the surplus pound notes rather than hand them over to the Government. That way at least you are making a tiny reduction in the amount of money in circulation, and thus in the rate of inflation.

The second rule is that the best advice is always the cheapest, not only in the long run but in the short run as well. I never cease to be amazed at the number of people who run businesses without any recourse to an accountant. No economy, even in the hardest of times, is more short-sighted than this. There are good accountants and indifferent ones, of course, as in any profession, but unless you have a quite exceptional knowledge of the highways and byways of tax legislation, any accountant worth his salt should be able to save you at least his fee before he turns round. There is the added, and important point, that a great deal depends on what inspectors of taxes will and will not accept, and how they interpret the figures you put before them. An accountant or tax adviser will have the advantage of being known to the taxation authorities. He will know the way their minds work. Equally important, they will often be prepared to accept unhesitatingly from him figures that they might query on your unsupported word, for the simple reason that he is, in a sense, backing you by putting his professional reputation at stake. Then on specific points it is possible to get advice from professional bodies. The Institute of Directors, for example, runs a taxation advice service for its members; I would like to think, though I am very far from convinced, that anyone who was a member of that august body would not be in the habit of neglecting tax matters. And, the *Sunday Telegraph* runs a taxation advisory service, retaining an eminent firm of City accountants to advise on replying to its readers' letters. It is, unfortunately, necessary to make a charge of £1 for each query, but this is very far below the actual cost of the service. It is also worth making unhesitating use of any services your bank provides.

At the top of the scale there are specialist firms that operate almost as financial supermarkets, offering a complete range of financial planning services to their clients, but those in need of such expertise hardly need telling by me.

At the opposite end of the scale from the clients of the large planning services come those people with small incomes and relatively uncluttered affairs. Even here, where every penny counts so much, it is relatively rare for it not to be possible for some improvement to be made. Somebody making a small, furnished letting, for example, may not be claiming what they might in terms of depreciation of furniture and fittings, or allowances on new items of equipment bought. In the last resort there is no reason not to use the Inland Revenue as unpaid tax advisers, asking to see the tax inspector and getting him to check that everything allowable has been claimed.

In sheer terms of numbers, though, the most important group is the middle range of people, in particular, the host of small or one-man businesses who are not as well served or as well informed as they might be. How many of the self-employed or people not in pension schemes are aware that they can get full tax relief on contributions to buy retirement annuities, i.e. private pensions? If they are under sixty years of age, they can invest up to £2,250 a year, or 15 per cent of their non-pensionable earnings completely tax-free to buy a retirement annuity. If they are more than sixty years of age the upper limit is relaxed and can go as high as £3,000 or 20 per cent. In these days of inflation, when the upper rates of tax begin to bite sooner and sooner in real terms, this is an immensely valuable concession, since what you are saving is tax at your highest rate. In these uncertain times, many people running their own businesses may be reluctant to undertake fresh financial commitments; they may feel they are not sure that their income will continue, or they may even be facing cash-flow problems. But the beauty of these retirement annuity plans, or at any rate of the better ones, is that you do not have to commit yourself to a contract to pay in a fixed sum year by year. You can pay in what you can afford, so that in a bad year you could omit payment altogether, or in an exceptionally good year increase it up to the maximum allowable for your age.

It is true that to undertake such a form of saving involves making one act of faith – that inflation will not be permitted to increase to the level where the value of all monetary savings is destroyed. However, in spite of the warnings earlier in this book, things are not yet at a pass where it is prudent to say 'Save nothing. Spend everything you have got.' Even in a time of relatively rapid inflation, at any point short of pure hyper-inflation, savings are needed as a cushion against hardship. Indeed it has been observed that there has been a tendency for overall savings to increase during the past two years or so. This is perfectly rational behaviour to anyone except a particularly blinkered sort of economist. To anyone facing possible unemployment or hardship, it is better to have money in the bank, even in depreciated and depreciating pounds, than no money at all.

This does, however, lead me to my third point: hedge against inflation where you can. This is not an argument for buying any of the dubious objects, from postage stamps to collections of Winston Churchill's works, often touted as 'hedges against inflation'. Many of these are things that you would find singularly hard to sell if ever you needed the money urgently, and even where they can be sold readily, the margin between buying and selling prices tends to be so large that a very big rise in value is required before you as much as break even.

There are three practicable inflation hedges that the ordinary man should be very much aware of. The first is one that most people are already aware of, the owner-occupied house. Belief in this may have taken a knock over the past two years as house prices have tumbled from their peak, but on any long-term view this is the shrewdest form of saving, provided only that the purchaser is satisfied that he can keep up with the outgoings. Since the market fell, very few people are trading up, but for anyone fortunate enough to have the cash to plough in, this is a very good time to do so since larger houses are down as much as 50 per cent from their peak. House prices do not rise in a steady line, but it is very rare for there to be a correction of this size. When economic circumstances improve – and I refuse absolutely to believe that they never will – or upon a change of Government, there could be a very sharp turn in the market. One can also hope that the £25,000 tax relief limit on mortgages will be amended or removed. The reasons why house purchase is incomparably the best investment remain what they always were: that the tax concessions on mortgage interest greatly lower the true cost of borrowing, and that building societies offer borrowers a uniquely favourable bargain. They take not a penny of any increase in the value of the property, while in any inflationary age the real value of the debt steadily decreases.

The second inflation hedge is nothing more nor less than gold. On the Continent, France in particular, where they are used to more disturbed conditions and more ruinous inflation than the British are, it is automatic for part of any portfolio to be kept in gold. Here again, as far as the British are concerned, we have seen too sharp a boom followed by a sharp drop in the price of gold. As so often, too many people were attracted into the market for the first time close to the very top and with the fall since then have doubtless decided that gold is a very bad investment. The fact remains that it has trebled in value over the past few years, and it is now recovering once again. I am not talking, however, of the possibility of making a quick profit (or loss), but of a prudent investment for the long term, and precaution against the possibility of inflationary chaos. Gold, of course, may not be held by residents of the U.K. Gold shares may be, but they face the risk of South Africa's uncertain future. Krugerrands (especially minted South African gold coins) may be held by U.K. residents and are probably the best answer.

For those to whom gold seems too exotic an investment, and indeed to everyone who wants to save, I most strongly recommend the Government's new inflation-proofed savings schemes. One of them, which everyone can take advantage of, is an extension of the S.A.Y.E. (Save As You Earn) scheme. Up to £20 a month can be invested. It bears no interest, but at the end of five years will be repaid in the form of a sum adjusted upwards in line with the change in the official cost of living index. If held for a further two years thereafter there is a bonus. The other scheme is for a lump sum investment of up to £500 by people of retirement age. Both these are only suitable for people who definitely will not require the money for at least five years, but no other savings medium can really compare. The first year of operation showed a rise in the cost of living index approximating 20 per cent; even if it were to be half this, there are few other ways of getting 10 per cent tax free. These schemes are not much publicized, and indeed the fact that the lump sum one is confined to the elderly suggests that the Government is extremely conscious of its overwhelming attractions, and is, in effect, rationing it. Elsewhere I have discussed the attractions of indexation as a defence against inflation. There is no doubt that the demand for indexed savings is likely to grow, and if after this book appears new indexed schemes are devised, the reader should certainly take advantage of them. The only danger they may incur is that such schemes are liable to tempt the Government to tamper with the cost of living index in order to keep it down, by artificially depressing the price of items figuring in the index, while letting other goods, not in the official index, rise. The temptation grows stronger when it is anxious to show that its counter-inflation policies are working. One should be aware of this, but public and Parliamentary alertness should stop this tendency going too far.

As far as individual taxes are concerned, it would take a book in itself to give any detailed advice. I can recommend the *Hambro Tax Guide*, which has the eminent Professor G. S. A. Wheatcroft as a Consulting Editor, as one excellent source of information. It is revised annually and the current (1976/7) edition is published by Robert Yeatman Ltd, and costs £4·50.

It is, however, worth making a few brief points about each major tax in turn. If even one person is saved a substantial sum as a result, who can say it is not worthwhile?

Income Tax

Apart from the need to check one's allowances, the most useful principle here is to have one's earned income coming from more than one source, and as far as possible to establish an occupation, even a part-time one, that can legitimately be assessed under Schedule D rather than Schedule E. This is because the expenses rule under Schedule D, the schedule applied to the self-employed, is less impossibly restrictive and onerous than that applied to Schedule E, which refers to income from employment. Under Schedule E only expenses 'wholly, necessarily and exclusively' incurred in one's occupation are allowable. Under Schedule D the words are 'wholly and exclusively', which, within proper limits, makes you the judge of what you need to spend to run your business. For example, if you run a business at home, you can quite properly charge a proportion of your home expenses including rates, lighting, heating, even care of the garden, against tax. If you take work home from the office, and spend just as many hours working at home, none of this is allowable.

Some people think this shows that Schedule D is too lax. My own view is that the word 'necessarily' in Schedule E is far too restrictive in view of the extreme difficulty of showing that a disbursement was absolutely necessary to do the job. Before he came to office, Mr Denis Healey fulminated against the self-employed and their alleged tax privileges, but he has taken no action so far (who knows, he may have learned a *little* wisdom?), and, following the dictum by Lord Clyde quoted earlier, one must arrange one's affairs to their best advantage.

Capital Gains Tax

This is, of course, iniquitous, since, in times of inflation, one is paying tax on paper profits that amount to real losses. One's only hope is to be alert to the ways in which it can be saved. If not more than £1,000 of chargeable assets are sold in any one year, no gains tax is payable. Moreover, instead of paying gains tax at 30 per cent, it is permissible as an alternative to take half the gain at your top rate of income tax (subject to various limits). Thus, if a self-employed person happens to have a very low income in any one year, that is clearly the year to realize a prospective capital gain. Finally, it is important to remember that losses can be carried forward but not backwards. This means that it is no good making a capital profit in one year and realizing a capital loss in the next, though the other way round is all right. Thus, if you have a sizeable capital gain in any one year, it is well worth seeing if there are any losses which you can establish *in the same year*.

Capital Transfer Tax

There is a firm pledge by Mrs Thatcher, the Conservative leader, to repeal this tax. The best advice, therefore, is to stay alive till the Conservatives get back. Since this is not really within one's direct control (we all would if we could), it is necessary to take some precautions while waiting for her to gallop to the rescue. As a general introduction I can, without a hint of impartiality, recommend *Capital Transfer Tax and You* (obtainable from Dept T, *Sunday Telegraph*, Fleet Street, London EC4, at 50p plus 10p postage). Thereafter there are innumerable guides flowing from the presses.

The main point in the meantime is, as always, to take advantage of any exemptions there are. Gifts totalling up to £2,000 can be made in any one year without incurring Capital Transfer Tax and the £2,000 can be carried forward for one year (i.e. nothing one year, £4,000 the next). In addition, you could, if you were so minded, make gifts of up to £100 to as many people as you like in any one year. Parents can give up to £5,000 as a marriage gift to each of their children, grandparents £2,500, others £1,000.

If you are quite, quite sure that your marriage is stable, there is a lot to be said for equalizing your assets between husband and wife. It is true that gifts between husband and wife are exempt, but if you simply leave your wife all your property then when she dies she is liable to pay much more tax than if your two estates were equal, and you each leave whatever you have to leave to your children. In addition, if your wife does not have funds of her own, you can make gifts to her that enable her to make use of the annual exemptions in *her* giving, say, to the children.

Owners of farms and businesses should be certainly taking advice. It may be prudent to start providing sums for possible tax by means of life assurance policies. In the case of some types of business, particularly those offering a service, it may be possible to run your business down and let your son start to build a new one up in his own name, even if he steals your customers. The more fanciful means of avoidance, such as being sued by your son for libel, or marrying your son's fiancée on your deathbed, belong, alas, only to the realm of fantasy.

Wealth Tax

The main hope must be that this will never be enacted. There is something to be said for a Wealth Tax at a moderate rate as an alternative to Capital Gains Tax, the Investment Income Surcharge and the present top rates of Income Tax. If a Wealth Tax is added, as Mr Healey apparently would like to do, to these existing imposts, we are entering the realms of explicit confiscation. Fortunately the practical problems are formidable. Without widespread exemptions it will be unworkable; but providing exemptions means creating loopholes. Problems of valuation are difficult while money would have to be drawn out of a business to pay the tax just when more investment is needed. Above all it must be remembered that no country with a Wealth Tax has remotely our existing weight of taxes; without one, Britain is more heavily taxed than any country that has one. Nor does imposing a Wealth Tax mean the redistribution of wealth; it cannot make the poor a penny better off, and other taxes may have to be increased to make up for the savings lost. This could be the last ditch in which we have to fight.

In sum there is no doubt that the tax system, which has been built up in an *ad hoc* fashion throughout this century, is in urgent need of reform. It is not satisfactory to have a system that so discourages thrift and is so onerous that whatever else falters, the profession of tax lawyer booms. We have already discussed the need for indexation, and the case for cutting the higher rates of tax. There is, too, a strong case – which has its supporters on the left as well as the right – for preferring to tax expenditure rather than income. This will actually encourage saving, unlike the present system which actively discourages it. What one seeks is not some elaborate Expenditure Tax, complete with all the apparatus of bureaucracy, but a gradual shift towards indirect rather than direct taxation. In the meantime the middle class must protect itself as best it can. The dice are loaded against the taxpayer but there is no ethical virtue in paying a penny more than you must.

15 Conclusion – agenda for action

The long haul is nearly done, and it remains only to bind together the themes of this book. In my days as a financial consultant I used to think that the most important single question I could ask anyone who came to me for advice was: where do you hope to be in five years' time? The answer I received defined the nature of my client's ambition, whether it was boundless or distinctly finite, and thus defined the nature of the answer he ought to receive. I also found that, in many cases, perhaps the majority, there was only one answer. The client knew what needed to be done, but when I told him to do it, in some way it lifted the responsibility from his shoulders.

It is time for the middle class to ask itself where it hopes to be in five years' time, or at any rate for its members to ask themselves that question. They can then go on to consider where they are likely to be in five years' time. The theme of this book has been that the answers to these two questions are very far apart, and that only a conscious resolve to fight back is likely to make any difference. There is a phrase from one of Winston Churchill's speeches that has been much in my mind as I have been writing this book. Speaking in Parliament on the Munich agreement in 1938, he said: 'This is only the first sip, the first foretaste of a bitter cup which will be proffered to us, year by year, unless by a supreme recovery of moral health and martial vigour we arise again and take our stand for freedom as in the olden time.' To me it defines precisely the frame of mind in which the middle class should prepare for what could be its last battle. Martial vigour in its strict sense may not be required – there is nothing in this book about private armies and the like – but I am sure that it is only by the exertion of moral strength that the middle class, which has always stood for freedom, will be able to continue to do so in the future. It has to have the moral strength to say, 'Thus far and no further.'

As, in the course of my writing, I have discussed these themes with friends, their comments have raised other fascinating subtopics. Why is 'bourgeois' a term of abuse, not just among the neo-Marxists and the sociological fraternity, but among sections of the middle class itself? It may be true that the upper class is negligible in numbers, but in terms of the 'establishment' does it not wield considerable power? In terms of social attitude, is the great divide between those who send their children away to school and those who do not? Has the concept of U and non-U speech any place in my categorizations? I have waxed eloquent about the middle class as the transmitter of culture; what about middle-class philistinism, which so many great authors have mercilessly dissected?

These are all the type of questions the English, or at any rate the English middle class, love to discuss. They are side-issues, interesting in themselves but not, I think, germane to the main issue; this is no time, either nationally or at this point of the book, to pursue even the most enticing of hares. There are, however, two questions that formed part of this list which I think I should confront.

The first is this: what do foreigners mean when they claim, as many of them do, that Britain is a class-ridden society, and are they right? This is a comment most often heard on the lips of Germans and Americans, both of whom, in post-war terms, are part of rootless, thrusting societies, and highly prosperous ones. It is not said nearly so much by Frenchmen or Italians, and I think in part it reflects the reaction of groups whose status is defined in terms of success, to a more orderly and settled tradition. In part it reflects high-wage economies looking down at a relatively low-wage economy. Does a German or American secretary have a higher status than a British secretary, or is it simply that she is conspicuously better paid? In short, I don't believe that it is wholly or even largely true. It does, however, have a nugget of truth or, at any rate, a truthful observation buried within it. Our industrial society, the factories that foreign businessmen are likely in this context to be particularly aware of, are in many cases frozen into attitudes stemming from far earlier stages of industrial society. Different treatment of white-collar and shopfloor workers, different starting times for management, these things, summed up perhaps in the classic case of the factory with *five* different levels of canteen, are the things that impress.

It is a moot point where the blame should be apportioned for this. In a society that draws so much of its strength from traditions, many of them of great value, bad traditions will tend to persist besides good ones. And I have no doubt that the development of working-class militancy in the form of our particular trade union movement, which is so deeply conservative with a small 'c', has had the effect of sharpening class consciousness and freezing attitudes that should have melted long ago.

This leads to the second question, a more personal one, but very relevant to the attitudes and future of the middle class. How, a friend wanted to know, did I personally become disillusioned with a Labour Party which I had warmly supported as a young man? It would be easy to point to specific points of disillusionment – anguish, for example, at the economic mismanagement of 1965, which now seems no more than a dress rehearsal for 1974. And yet there were two deeper causes. I had always been interested in wealth-creation and found the Labour Party, obsessed as it is with problems of distribution, increasingly unsympathetic on this. Above all, in my green and salad days, I had believed that socialism acted to strengthen the unselfish and generous impulses in people. It became increasingly obvious that the trade union bureaucracy, which no doubt had stemmed from originally generous impulses, had become a monster of selfishness, and that the altruistic talk of the intellectuals of the Labour movement acted as a by no means opaque cover for far less attractive impulses, though I would not deny for a moment the presence of countless thousands of kind and generous individuals in the Labour Party. Experience teaches: I also became more and more doubtful about the virtues and efficiency of widespread State intervention.

The question is whether all this is inherent in socialism as such, or whether it is merely a question of the particular form that social democracy has taken in this country. To my mind, the fact that we have a monolithic Labour Party backed by a mono-lithic trade union movement has had a disastrous effect in many ways. It has given the far left a legitimacy that, on the whole, it does not have in Continental Europe. It has also tainted the attitudes of the Labour right. They have always had to compete with the left in their own party, often they have had to surrender issues of principle for the sake of party unity, and worst of all they have had to develop their own ideology to compete with the left. That is why, alone among European social-democratic parties, the Labour Party in Britain has an ideological right wing, relentlessly pursuing its egalitarian fallacies, as well as an ideological left wing.

This is not intended to be a book about politics but it is impossible to discuss the middle class without discussing political attitudes. Conservative Governments, as we have seen, have been by no means particularly helpful to the middle class, but next to inflation, it is programmes adopted by the Labour Party that directly threaten its destruction. Yet, as we know, something like one third of the middle class habitually votes Labour. That is its privilege and its right. But for the future it must either do so with its eyes open, conscious that it is voting for its own euthanasia or it must demand a Labour Party that reflects its interests as sincerely as it tries to forward the interests of the organized sections of workers.

This is not quite such a pipe-dream as it seems. The political market place has many imperfections, not the least of which is that, in voting for one thing or many things that he wants, the elector also finds himself voting for things that he does not want in the least. But political parties want to gain power, they are responsive, in however clumsy a fashion, to the tides of public opinion. There is another point. Elections are often discussed by psephologists and the like in terms which suggest that the result is determined by shifts in opinion on the part of a very small number of 'floating voters'. This is a complete misunderstanding. There are great sub-oceanic tides of opinion beneath an apparently placid surface, with many millions of votes shifting one way or the other; it is only the net result of these massive shifts that shows in the so-called 'swing'. I would like one of those shifts, the shift of middle-class opinion, to become visible and therefore effective in terms of policies as well as of election results.

One has only to talk to senior members of the Parliamentary Labour Party to discover what deep unhappiness there is about its programmes, its attitudes – and a fair number of its personalities – among many who have given a life-time to its service. As an outsider I can go one step further than them and say that if I were a Labour Party supporter I would want my party to have a long period in the wilderness to restructure itself and regain its soul. In the short term, such a development would also be the best hope of the middle class.

In the longer term the middle class will only survive if it deserves to survive. The main message of this book has been that it should have a good conceit of itself. It has nothing to apologize for, nothing to be ashamed of, except, perhaps, its reluctance till now to act as an effective pressure group.

Because this book has a practical purpose I have been particularly pleased to see it, in its original form, so sympathetically received. To my surprise, out of a very large number of reviews only two rejected its main thesis and only one was downright hostile. Quite a number of reviewers offered helpful and constructive ideas. One or two admittedly regretted that I had used the term 'middle class' to cover a group of attitudes that, valuable as they were, had no need to be described in terms of class. The only reply to this is that people who hate and despise those attitudes unhesitatingly describe them as 'middle class'; the label may be inadequate, but it cannot be discarded if the values are to be preserved.

Perhaps the most thought-provoking contribution came from Mr Roy Lewis, writing in *The Times*. He suggested that there have always been two streams in the middle class, one going up, one coming down. The Victorian age was the great time of the entrepreneur, the self-made man establishing himself in prosperity. In contrast clerks were lowly people, little esteemed. Now, he suggested, the thrusting sections of the middle class rose safely to prosperity in the State sector, especially the Civil Service, and it was the entrepreneurs who were less and less regarded and found it harder and harder to get on.

It is difficult to quarrel with this description. I will only add that a middle class which completely lost its independence and became synonymous with the bureaucracy would bear little relation to the independent, and independently minded, section of the community whose values I seek to preserve. It would still be the death of the middle class by another name.

The main point economically is that the middle class has to assert and re-assume its wealth-creating role, to the benefit of the whole community. The alternative is a steady progression to a kind of economic slumdom, which we are finding foreshadowed in so many public services, such as the Health Service, today. If we do not succeed, and if the middle class finally abdicates, Britain is not likely to turn, as the more sanguine sort of socialist theorist hopes, into a superior kind of Sweden. It is much more likely to finish up, as far as economic standards are concerned, a less efficient sort of Yugoslavia, or an even less dynamic version of Hungary.

Where we shall end up if all the things I have hoped for in this book come to pass is more difficult to say, if only because the restoration of economic dynamism is, in itself, so profound a change that it vastly extends the range of options and possibilities before us. With expectations no longer continually disappointed it will certainly be a happier, more open, less envious and less discontented society. I would not expect, and I would not want, a middle-class life-style to become universal, though I hope that middle-class standards of comfort might. Evidence from societies rapidly growing in affluence, such as Germany, suggests that an increasingly prosperous working class becomes more rather than less proud of its own standards and values and way of life. That is as it should be. One of the cornerstones of middle-class values is a belief in choice, and that includes freedom to choose how one wishes to live. It is by extending prosperity and extending choice that the middle class transcends its own concentration upon material things.

References

Chapter 1

1. Roy Lewis and Angus Maude, *The English Middle Classes*, Phoenix House, 1949.
2. Mark Abrams, 'Social Class and Politics', in *Class*, ed. Richard Mabey, Anthony Blond, 1967.
3. John Raynor, *The Middle Class*, Longmans, 1969.
4. Tom Punt, 'Social Pressures', in *Britain in the 1980s*, ed. James Morrell, The Henley Centre for Forecasting, 1975.
5. Raymond Postgate, 'Class in Britain and Abroad', in Mabey, op. cit.
6. Gallup Poll, 1948.
7. Taylor Nelson & Associates, Monitor Survey.
8. Jack Jones, 'The Case against Percentages', in *New Statesman*, 5 September 1975.

Chapter 3

9. Royal Commission on the Distribution of Income and Wealth, Report No. 1, Initial Report on the Standing Reference, 1975.
10. ibid., Report No. 4, Second Report on the Standing Reference, 1976.
11. ibid., Report No. 1, 1975.
12. Raynor, op. cit.
13. Inland Revenue figures.
14. Submission to the Diamond Commission, made available to the author.

Chapter 4

15. *The Economist*, 17 May 1975.
16. *Accountant*, 10 July 1975.

Chapter 5

17. *The Economist*, 18 May 1974.

Chapter 6

18. Source: *National Income and Expenditure Blue Book*, H.M.S.O., 1975 ed. Earlier figures from A. T. Peacock and Jack Wiseman, *The Growth of Public Expenditure in the U.K.*, Allen & Unwin, 1967.

Chapter 7

19. John Vaizey, 'Why Equality?', in *Whatever Happened to Equality?*, ed. John Vaizey, B.B.C., 1975.
20. Ralph Miliband, *The State in Capitalist Society*, Weidenfeld & Nicolson, 1969.
21. Anthony Crosland, *Socialism Now and Other Essays*, Jonathan Cape, 1974.
22. S. Brittan, *The Economic Contradictions of Democracy*, paper presented to the British Association at Sterling, 1974.
23. W. G. Runciman and A. H. Halsey, 'Class Status and Power', in Vaizey, op. cit.

Chapter 8

24. *Guardian*, 11 November 1975.
25. *Guardian*, 12 November 1975.
26. *Sunday Telegraph*, 2 November 1975.

Chapter 11

27. Ralph Harris, 'Co-operation through Competition', in *1985: An Escape from Orwell's 1984*, ed. Dr Rhodes Boyson, Churchill Press, 1975.
28. *Where Do Pay Rises Come From?*, Working Together, 1973.

Chapter 12

29. Raynor, op. cit.
30. Norman St John-Stevas and Leon Brittan, *How to Save Your Schools*, Conservative Political Centre.

More about Penguins
and Pelicans

Penguinews, which appears every month, contains details of all the new books issued by Penguins as they are published. From time to time it is supplemented by *Penguins in Print*, which is our complete list of almost 5,000 titles.

A specimen copy of *Penguinews* will be sent to you free on request. Please write to Dept EP, Penguin Books Ltd, Harmondsworth, Middlesex, for your copy.

In the U.S.A.: For a complete list of books available from Penguins in the United States write to Dept CS, Penguin Books, 625 Madison Avenue, New York, New York 10022.

In Canada: For a complete list of books available from Penguins in Canada write to Penguin Books Canada Ltd, 2801 John Street, Markham, Ontario L3R 1B4.

New Penguin Fiction

The Family Arsenal

Paul Theroux

A novel of urban terror and violence set in the grimy decay of South-east London.

'One of the most brilliantly evocative novels of London that has appeared for years . . . very disturbing indeed' – Michael Ratcliffe in *The Times*

Billy Liar on the Moon

Keith Waterhouse

'I beg you, read this brilliant book. Even if you have to steal it' – *Sunday Mirror*

Billy Liar is back, older but not wiser. And his fantasies have come home to roost in the awful concrete jungle of Shepford. Surrounded by a wife, rat-faced neighbours, scheming rivals at work, and a lovely, sexy mistress whose tongue can do things Billy hasn't even thought of, he struggles with his *alter ego*, Oscar, to attain a semblance of adulthood.

The Penguin Dorothy Parker

The Penguin Dorothy Parker includes stories and poems published collectively in 1944; later uncollected stories, articles and reviews; and the contents of *Constant Reader* (her *New Yorker* book reviews) – in all of which she sharpens her legendary wits on the foibles of others.

The Great Railway Bazaar

Paul Theroux

Paul Theroux set out one day with the intention of boarding every train that chugged into view from Victoria Station in London to Tokyo Central – and so began a hugely entertaining railway odyssey.

Evelyn Waugh

Christopher Sykes

'It is a definitely not to be missed if you are interested in Evelyn Waugh, his work, the art of biography, or even the personality of one of our great English eccentrics' – Antonia Fraser

The Liners

Terry Coleman

The liners of the North Atlantic run, with their opulent luxury and fabulous clientele, fired the imagination of millions in their day. Terry Coleman stokes the flame anew with this beautiful book.

Superwoman

Shirley Conran

'This historic volume' (as the *Guardian* put it) is a practical guide to running a home in ways that minimize the chores and save time and money. It is aimed especially at women who have to combine that job with earning a living outside the home.